A HISTORY OF

FOOTBALL

This new and revised edition first published in the UK in 2004
by Green Umbrella exclusively for
Sutton Publishing · Phoenix Mill · Thrupp · Stroud · Gloucestershire · GL5 2BU

First published in the UK in 2003

© Green Umbrella Publishing 2004

British Library Cataloguing in Publication Data
A catalogue record for this book is available from the British Library

Printed and bound in Hong Kong

ISBN 0 7509 3953 2

A HISTORY OF
FOOTBALL

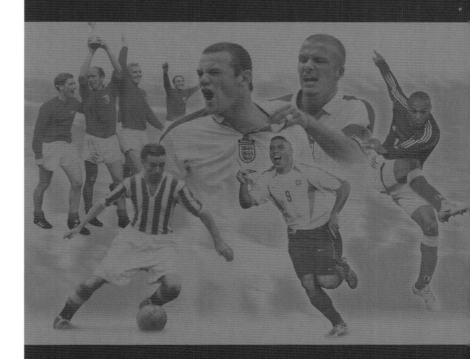

Origins of the Game

The First Golden Age

The Post-war UK Boom

Premier Passions

Football Goes Global

The Future of Football

A HISTORY OF
FOOTBALL

**England's
Finest Hour**

**Total
Football**

**Alan Green's
First XI**

TABLE OF CONTENTS

ALAN GREEN

FOREWORD

When you watch as much football every season as I do, then either I'm off my head or I'm head over heels in love with the game. My wife says that it's both. I know it's definitely the latter.

Alan Green
August 2004

I realise this particularly on cold wet winter's evenings at obscure venues when the commentary position is wretched, which is surprisingly often, and they've run out of tea at half-time in the pressroom. At times like that I do ask myself: "What am I doing here?" Then I have a laugh remembering something that's happened that was especially awful (you do have to laugh) or I smile with pleasure recalling a special goal. Every football fan has bottomless 'lows' as well as incredible highs, frequently in the same game.

And that's what I am – a fan, albeit with a microphone. I don't really have a career. No, it's a magnificent hobby for which I'm also handsomely paid – or reasonably so.

Being a football commentator is wonderfully privileged. I think back to the 1994 World Cup Final between Brazil and Italy in Pasadena, California. The match itself was woeful and was rapidly dispatched to the outer reaches of my memory bank. What I do recall is sitting in my elevated commentary seat no more than ten yards behind the podium on which sat the trophy itself. I could almost touch it. How many have had that experience?

However much I love the sport, I never fail to recognise its problems. I was commentating at the FA Cup semi-final at Hillsborough in 1989 when so many Liverpool supporters tragically lost their lives. It was an experience that radically changed my own life and the perspective through which I view the game. The old 'Shanklyism' that football isn't a matter of life and death, "it's more important than that", was never more inappropriate.

So many of football's current ills stem from placing too much importance on what should always be remembered is simply a sport. Yes, it touches our lives in so many different ways. For many people it is their life, deciding their moods, influencing what they do. But passion for the game, and I bow to no-one in my passion for football, should never trip over into hooliganism – an ailment that remains as big a problem in football as its rampant over commercialisation.

I hope you enjoy this book. I'm sure you'll disagree with some of what you read. Watching and enjoying football, after all, is about opinion as much as it is about knowledge. Some of you will laugh at my World XI (remember, my choice was of players that I'd actually 'seen in the flesh'). Just so long as you laugh…

Origins
of the Game

Chapter
ONE

Origins of the Game

It is now well over a century since association football – also commonly known as soccer, to differentiate it first from rugby football, then American football – was first played in an organised fashion, much longer since the Romans played a ball-based contact sport. Yet here in the 21st Century the game retains its position as the most popular in the world.

Its appeal surely remains its simplicity. It can be improvised almost anywhere by any number of players, and requires a simple, spherical ball rather than a specially shaped one. It has been played by people of limited stature, five feet or less, and occasionally those of excessive height or weight. And with the objective simply to score a goal between two posts, rolled up coats or other markers, its rules are more easily comprehensible than most of its rivals.

Answering the question as to where the game originated is more difficult. The Chinese are recorded to have played *tsu chu* – *tsu* meaning to kick and *chu* a stuffed leather ball. The Japanese meanwhile played *kemari,* a game of eight players apiece played on a pitch some 14 metres square, the boundaries marked by four trees – a willow, cherry, pine and maple.

The games may in fact be related, since early sporting contact between the countries was recorded. Elsewhere, Mexico justified their double selection as twentieth-century World Cup hosts by mixing the skills of football with those of basketball, setting hoops on a wall to form goals for the rival teams to aim at.

As previously mentioned, the first football in Britain may well have been imported with the invading Romans. *Harpustum,* a Roman word for 'handball', was an individual ball game with physical contact very much part and parcel of it, and was developed from the rather more genteel Ancient Greek *episkyros.* The legions may well have played this as they awaited their return to sunnier climes. Back in Italy, the game developed into the sixteenth-century *calcio,* with teams of 26 or 27 players apiece, typically wearing green or red colours. These games were often the subject of much money changing hands on the touchline. The rules, *discorsa calcio,* were formalised around 1580.

As the translation of *harpustum* suggests, however, these were games more akin to today's rugby than modern football. Yet the two modern games developed from a common root, only to be divided in nineteenth-century England. And, perhaps surprisingly for a game now associated with the working classes, this division and codification of association football took place in the public schools where the upper classes sent their children to be turned into young gentlemen.

Britain can claim to have developed and formalised the rules of association football which, by and large, still hold sway the world over. Yet prior to its adoption by the gentry in the nineteenth century the game enjoyed a reputation as the sport of hooligans and rabble-rousers, with the participants in the average game outnumbering the crowds at many English lower-division games today. Several fixtures in the early history of football attained the status of annual rituals, being recorded in written works and art. The Shrove Tuesday contest at Ashbourne, Derbyshire, celebrates one of the earliest recorded indigenous football games. With one half of the town pitted against the other (what price Merseyside, Glasgow or Manchester?), the goals are the parish church at one end and the gates of Ashbourne Hall at the other. This bizarre 'fixture' was first recorded in the year AD 217, and continues to this day.

• **Opposite**
A game of eighteenth-century street football, where few rules prevailed.

• **Above**
Boys play an informal game of football, circa 1850.

• **Above**
Football matches have often coincided with festivals. William Howitt's drawing depicts a rough and tumble fixture on Easter Monday 1750.

The game had spread its roots far and wide even by that time: Dorset's Corfe Castle and Scone in Scotland were among other venues where an annual Shrove Tuesday fixture was observed. At Chester, a leather ball was introduced (appropriately courtesy of the town's cobblers), the City Hall and the hall at Rodehoe being the goals. Few, however, played on pitches such as the one recorded in Cornwall in 1602, whose goals were three to four miles apart and the teams were each comprised of the menfolk of two or three neighbouring parishes! London was at the forefront of these 'mob football' games, perhaps the only ones where the hooligans took an active part. The meat market at Smithfield was a favoured venue for the apprentices to gather in numbers up to 500-strong, while Cheapside, Covent Garden and the genteel suburb of Kingston Upon Thames were among the other noted venues.

With few rules prevailing and uncontrollable numbers of players in action, the risk of permanent injury was high. Scores could be (and doubtless were) settled during the course of such games, and there was an inevitable backlash from authority. Kings, the clergy, the womenfolk, even the Puritans, all attempted to have the game banned...without success. Football has always had its critics. The game has often been seen as a source of national pride and a peaceful way of settling scores. In 1365, however, King Edward III had exactly the opposite situation on his hands when it became apparent his soldiers would rather play football than fight. The inevitable ban is said to have improved their archery, but failed to stamp out the game. Indeed, a contemporary carving in Gloucester Cathedral shows two fourteenth-century footballers vying for possession – surely an indication that the game was nearing acceptability.

When Cambridge University introduced it into the curriculum at the turn of the seventeenth century, even its detractors had to reconsider. But with a

welter of different rules proliferating, these games were strictly intramural affairs. With the advent of the Industrial Revolution, few of the downtrodden working classes had the time or energy to pursue such a physically demanding sport, and football passed into the hands of the leisured upper classes.

Each school seemed to have its own special set of rules, often tailored to conform to the surface on which the game was played. At Charterhouse, where the stony cloisters provided the pitch for 20 players a side, the ball was played by feet alone; at Rugby, handling (but not running in possession) was positively encouraged. Harrow played a recognisable form of today's game on grass, 11 players making up a team, while Winchester's goals extended the entire length of the goal line, like rugby's try line today.

This situation would not last. The catalyst for change and standardisation was William Webb Ellis's legendary dash with the ball in 1823 that eventually gave rise to the game of rugby. This form of football broke ranks with soccer in 1848, when a 14-man committee at Cambridge University defined the game as permitting handling only to control the ball. Further rules then stated that the goals should consist of two posts.

Fouls were defined as tripping, kicking or holding, and an offside rule insisting on three men between the passer and the opposing goal was instituted. Football had arrived and, when the Sheffield Cricket Club permitted matches to be

played on their Bramall Lane pitch in the late 1850s, it seemed the game was almost respectable. Sheffield can thus claim to be Britain's oldest football club, although today they are firmly in the shadow of League giants Wednesday and United. Their players emanated from the city's Old Collegiate School. Games against local rivals such as Hallam (formed 1857) attracted 600 spectators, while their 1904 Amateur Cup win remains their greatest achievement.

• Above
A group of boys at play in the mid nineteenth century.

• Below
The first purpose-built boots were light-years away from today's lightweight designs.

• Above
A game at Rugby
School in 1845,
three years before
the handling code
broke away.

• Below
Association
football retained
the sphere while
rugby went
'egg-shaped'.

Such organisation was by no means confined to the North. The Blackheath Club formed in Kent in 1857, while others formed in the 1850s included Hampstead Heathens (playing, of course, on London's Hampstead Heath). The Old Harrovians were ex-pupils of Harrow School, while other Harrow old boys founded Wanderers, originally named Forest Football Club after their ground in Epping Forest near Snaresbrook. Notts County, established in 1862, were the first of the current Football League clubs to be founded. With such grassroots activity flourishing, the way was clear for an association of these teams to be formed.

The face of football has never been changed quite so radically as on 26 October 1863, when 11 southern English clubs each sent representatives to London's Freemason's Tavern in the west central district of Holborn. Their intent was to thrash out a commonly acceptable form of rules by which the game of football could be played. They adopted the following resolution: "That it is advisable that a football association should be formed for the purpose of settling a code of rules for the regulation of the game of football."

An annual general meeting of the Football Association, as it was termed, was set for the last

week in September, roughly setting the beginning of the traditional football season. All those clubs which were of at least a year's standing could send two representatives if their one guinea subscription was fully paid up. Not all those present, however, could give total backing to the movement. The Charterhouse representative, for instance, agreed with the broad aims of the association but felt he

C.W. Waddington.

T.W. Blenkiron.

C. Aubrey Smith.

W.N. Cobbold.

C. Wreford Brown.

"Weight must tell."

"An Athletic Celebrity."

"The Defender of the Fortress"

Saved!

Partisans.

S.T. Dadd

Union was formed in 1871 by those for whom handling and hacking held no fears.

The rules agreed by the FA included the maximum length and breadth of the pitch, the procedures for kicking off and defined terms such as a goal, throw-in and offside. Corners were effectively free kicks, taken 15 yards from the goal line opposite where the ball went out of play. The rugby tactic of 'making a mark' (catching the ball and making a mark with the heel to claim a free kick) remained. Passing the ball by hand was permitted if caught 'fairly or on the first bounce'. Yet even though nails, iron plates and *gutta percha* were banned from footwear, the rules were strangely non-specific in such matters as number of players, the penalty for foul play or even the shape of the ball. Such matters were to be decided by agreement between the captains.

had to wait to gauge the reaction of the other 'great schools' before giving up their own brand of the game. Harrow, too, were initially unwilling to change their home-grown rules.

The actual rules themselves were agreed by early December – and, fortunately for the reluctant Harrow representative, they were based on that school's understanding of how the game was played. Prior to this, however, impassioned discussion had led to the resignation of Rugby from the association, not on the issue of handling but on the question of 'hacking' or physically kicking opponents. The Rugby Football

Rudimentary and incomplete as these rules were in themselves, they had the immediate effect of stimulating competition. An annual New Year fixture between Sheffield and Nottingham was inaugurated on 2 January 1865, Nottingham (now Notts County), the oldest current League club, having been founded three years earlier. Sheffield ventured to London in the following year, but having won the first Nottingham fixture they then found themselves at the wrong end of a 4-0 scoreline. In 1865, Nottingham Forest were formed, and the first 'derby' game against local rivals County followed.

• *Above*
A composite illustration showing scenes and personalities from an FA Cup sixth-round tie between Old Carthusians and Preston North End in 1887. Preston won 2-1 after extra time.

Chesterfield (1866) and Stoke (1867) were next to join, and the game spread, no longer the exclusive preserve of the public schools yet by no means a working-class pastime. A crucial rule relaxed in 1867 was the provision that players in front of the ball were offside, thus reducing passing movements to lateral or backward directions. No wonder few goals were scored! This rule change took time to affect the pattern of play, which depended largely on individuals dribbling their way into a scoring position. Sheffield's game in London in 1866 had enabled the FA to observe their rules at close quarters. As a result, handling and catching the ball were soon abolished (save for the goalkeeper) and a tape was stretched between the posts (Sheffield's bar was introduced in 1882). But it was contact with the Scots who had developed their game well away from public school influence that was to broaden football's horizons rapidly.

The first FA Cup Final was contested in 1872, before 2,000 paying spectators, by Wanderers and Royal Engineers, the latter hot favourites. Injury, however, played a crucial part as it so often did in these pre-substitute days, and a broken collarbone sustained in the first few minutes by an Engineers player effectively put them at a disadvantage. Wanderers managed just one goal, but it was enough. This was scored by one AH Chequer, a pseudonym used by MP Betts to signify he had been a member of the Harrow Chequers old boys' team scheduled to face Wanderers in the first round. The team had scratched, hence Betts was not Cup-tied and ended up playing for his intended opponents!

The FA Cup was clearly the start of something big. Within a few years, all clubs wished to take part – and by doing so accepted the FA rules of football which remain the basis by which the game is played throughout the world today. The dominant teams in the Cup's early years were the 'Gentlemen' or southerners, with Old Etonians (6), Wanderers (5), Royal Engineers and Oxford University (both 4) clocking up most Final appearances in the first

dozen. Outside this Big Four, only four other sides managed to reach the final at all – Blackburn Olympic, Blackburn Rovers, Old Carthusians and Clapham Rovers. Wanderers notched the greatest number of wins, emerging victorious in all of their FA Cup Final appearances.

One of Wanderers' five Finals, in 1873, saw them play just a single game to win. This was the only season in which the FA Challenge Cup, to give it its full name, was played as a true challenge, the other teams playing each other for the right to throw down the gauntlet. Not unsurprisingly, Oxford University, the eventual challengers, were somewhat more fatigued than their opponents and succumbed 2-0, unusually choosing to play without a goalkeeper. Scottish team Queen's Park had withdrawn from the semi-final due to problems raising travel expenses, a decision that led directly to the formation of the Scottish FA.

Wanderers won the Cup in perpetuity after what remains one of only two hat-tricks of wins, between 1876 and 1878. The Cup was, however, returned to the Football Association on condition that no club

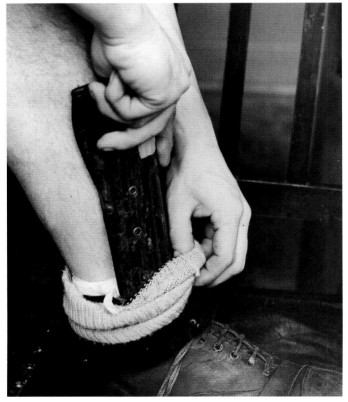

• **Opposite**
Old Corinthians footballer WR Moon epitomises the amateur game that held sway in the late nineteenth/early twentieth centuries.

• **Above**
The Royal Engineers team that won the first ever FA Cup Final, defeating Wanderers at the Kennington Oval in 1872.

• **Left**
Though the rules agreed in 1863 outlawed nails and iron plates in boots, shin protection has remained necessary.

17

could subsequently win it outright. Wanderers' main rivals in the 1870s were the Royal Engineers, who lost only twice (the Cup Finals of 1872 and 1874) in their 86 matches between 1871 and 1875. Their Major Marindin was later FA President and, after appearing in two losing FA Cup Finals, went on to referee a further eight

By the time the Football Association was formed in 1863, the teams had settled to 11 players apiece – and, with the obvious and notable exception of Rugby, it was accepted that only one player on either side, the goalkeeper, could handle the ball. As we will observe shortly, however, local variations still existed. Corner kicks from the intersection of touch and goal-line were generally introduced in 1872, although the Sheffield clubs had been using these for four years or so previously. Wing-halves (midfielders) typically fulfilled the corner-kicking responsibilities, handing over to wing-forwards around the turn of the century. As with children's playground football today, everyone wanted to be an attacker and the goalkeeper was typically covered by, at most, two defenders. Players bunched into thirds of the field, leaving wide open spaces unattended.

It was the Scots who first discovered the opportunities this offered, and their emphasis on team play saw them advance apace. They were also assisted by playing to consistent rules. The 2-3-5 formation evolved, with three of the forwards now dropping deeper as half-backs to provide an extra line of defence where necessary. The centre-half acted as the supply route to the front line. This 'pyramid' style of play was employed by the Double (League and FA Cup)-winning Preston team

• **Above**
Newcastle's Billy McCracken, whose tactics led to a change in the offside law.

in the League's first season, and their success spoke for itself.

One major problem with the offside rule was exploited by Newcastle defender Billy McCracken. He would move forward to play his opponents offside, knowing that there was still a covering man as well as the goalkeeper to foil the attacker even if he mistimed his run – which was not often. Other teams followed suit, and the result was games where the team in possession found themselves stopped at the half-way line. The balance was quite clearly wrong, and had to be tilted in favour of enterprising play.

Not surprisingly in view of past events, this was at the Scots' insistence. The new law simply removed a defending player from the equation. Now two players had to be between the man in possession and his opponents' goal line when the ball was played – a situation that left the defenders far less margin for error. Few were willing to risk exposing their goalkeeper, and those that did often paid the penalty. The change was an immediate success. In the season following the law change, the goal tally for the League's divisions rose from 4,700 to 6,373.

Penalties were introduced in September 1891 as a result of an incident in the previous season, during an FA Cup quarter final between Notts County and Stoke at Trent Bridge. County's Hendry produced an acrobatic goalkeeping save – unfortunately, however, he was the left-back. A free kick was awarded on the goal line, but goalkeeper Toone saved the point-blank shot. Since County's 1-0 win meant they

reached the semi-final and later the Final, a public outcry provoked a change in the laws.

By cruel irony, Stoke were also put at a disadvantage the following season when Aston Villa's goalkeeper kicked the ball out of the ground in disgust when Stoke were awarded a penalty. Since only two minutes remained on the referee's watch, there was insufficient time to retrieve the ball and Stoke, again losing 1-0, were denied the chance to save the game. Subsequent changes decreed that time should be added on to enable the penalty to be taken even if normal time had elapsed, while in 1892 the rules stated that a player could kick the ball only once before it had to be touched by another. This prevented the ball being dribbled into goal from the spot.

While football was changing its rules and regulations, playing kit was undergoing its own metamorphosis. In the 1870s, for instance, a match

• **Above**
Blackburn and Notts County contest the FA Cup Final in 1891, the season in which a quarter-final tie provoked the introduction of the penalty kick.

programme was essential for player identification, the colour of stockings or cap being the only differentiating feature between men of the same team. Although numbering was not introduced until 1933, caps had long since fallen into disuse.

Stimulated by the 1866 game with Sheffield, the London-based Football Association determined to expand the game's influence into a wider area. Sheffield themselves joined in 1867, and other teams were quick to follow suit. The amazing expansion of the 1870s was due primarily to the effort of one Charles Alcock, elected at the age of 28 as Secretary of the Association. He devised the idea of international competition, inaugurating an annual England-Scotland fixture. His address to the readers of the *Glasgow Herald,* advised them that the FA was to stage an international match at Kennington Oval, home of Surrey Cricket Club, on 19 November. Representatives were invited.

Captain of the team that emerged from this public appeal was Robert Smith, one of the three brothers instrumental in the formation of Queen's Park FC and now resident in London. His team, which lost 1-0 in the fixture, was composed entirely of Scots living south of the border (the reaction of the *Glasgow Herald's* readership remains unrecorded), but the stage had been set for three repeat encounters, in which the best Scotland could manage was a single 1-1 draw.

The balance of power was to shift noticeably, however, with the first international on Scottish soil (a goalless draw at the West of Scotland Cricket Club at Partick on 30 November 1872), and one of the most bitterly-disputed fixtures in the history of football was well and truly born. Meanwhile, Alcock had devised the ideal method of encouraging competitive play: the Football Association Cup, purchased for the princely sum of £20. Fifteen clubs

entered for the 1871-72 competition, though one – Donington Grammar School in Lincolnshire – withdrew without playing a game. Queen's Park, who contributed a guinea to the cost of the trophy, were lucky enough to draw Donington – then, thanks to a lopsided draw, contest the semi-finals without having had to play a single qualifying game.

Their semi-final against Wanderers (the team of which Alcock was secretary, and formerly known as Forest) was played in London, as indeed were all semis and Finals for the first years. The two teams could not break the goalless deadlock, and with extra time and penalty shootouts not yet devised, the Scots withdrew, being unable to manage the 800-mile round trip to Glasgow and back for the replay.

• **Above**
A scroll marking Charles Alcock's service to the Football Association as its first secretary.

The demise of Wanderers as strongest of the Gentlemen teams was mirrored by the rise of the public schools' 'old boy' teams. Two Old Etonians victories over them in 1878-79 and 1879-80 marked the turning of the tide. Their most famous player Arthur (later Lord) Kinnaird, a future FA President, chose to play for his old school rather than the team he'd represented previously. This was a significant loss, for Kinnaird was clearly the outstanding player of the era. He won five Cup winner's medals, as well as one cap for Scotland. After retiring from playing, he served as FA President for some 33 years.

Soon after the second defeat, Wanderers retired from competitive football completely. It was well that they did, for the game was about to be taken over by the 'professors', professional footballers from Scotland who lent their talents to such northern teams as Darwen, Sheffield Wednesday and Bolton. Professionalism reflected the industrial nature of the North, where leisure time was at a premium. The match that signified the end of the Gentlemen's monopoly was the Cup Final of 1882 when Blackburn became the first northern club to make it to the last stage of the contest. They were unlucky to lose 1-0 to Old Etonians, and indeed had been tipped to win.

Old Etonians' run of 31 wins and four draws is the longest ever unbeaten sequence in English first-class football. (Arsenal managed 30 League games in 2002.) Lord Kinnaird was the Etonians' captain, and he created history by standing on his head after receiving the Cup. The competition was about to be turned upside down, too: Old Etonians were the last amateur club to win the trophy, and no southern team was to write their name on it before the end of the century.

Three public parks existed in Glasgow. The keenest footballers gathered at Queen's Park, so it was not surprising that the leading club should bear that name. Queen's Park contested the FA Cup keenly until the SFA outlawed participation in 1887. They reached the Final twice, in 1884 and 1885: their opponents in each case were Blackburn Rovers, the scores 2-1 and 2-0. The first game was contentious in that referee Major Marindin disallowed two Queen's

• **Above**
Glasgow side Queen's Park were defeated by Blackburn Rovers in the 1884 English FA Cup Final, held at the Kennington Oval.

• **Above**
By 1899, when
Sheffield United
beat Derby
County in the
FA Cup Final,
football was a
civilised game.

Park goals for offside, due to confusion about which rule was being played. Blackburn went on to emulate Wanderers in winning the Cup three times in consecutive years, triumphing over West Bromwich after a replay. Their captain Jimmy Brown created a record in scoring in each of the three games. And though they could not now win the Cup in perpetuity, Blackburn returned to win again in 1890 and 1891. The professionals had taken over.

It may seem far-fetched, but the founder of the English Football League was not only a Scotsman but a man who never played a game of first-class football in his entire life. Perthshire gentleman William McGregor was the prime mover behind two meetings held in the spring of 1888 in London and Manchester involving the 12 football clubs who were to become the League's founder members. The London meeting took place on 22 March 1888 at Anderton's Hotel in London, on the eve of that year's Cup Final. The clubs' revenue depended on a good Cup run: an early exit could be financially disastrous, while postponements of friendly games due to Cup replays often meant fixtures were not fulfilled, resulting in an understandable lack of commitment from many spectators. Matters were completed on 17 April at the Royal Hotel in Manchester.

Curiously, McGregor originally thought the name Football League would be confused with the politically motivated Irish Land League, but that, by majority vote, was the name selected for this new competition that guaranteed fixtures and revenue for

the country's top dozen teams. Geographically speaking, these clubs were split equally between the North and the Midlands; the South of England remained a stronghold of the amateur game, and no professional football of note was played there.

Preston North End were the first Champions in the season 1888-89, with Aston Villa runners-up. So dominant were Preston, in fact, that they achieved the League and Cup double. What wrote their name into the record books, however, was the fact that they were undefeated in the League and did not concede a Cup goal – a record that seems likely never to be broken, given the number of fixtures it would now take a Premiership club to achieve the same feat. Their record in that first season bears repeating. Playing 22 matches, home and away, they won 18 and drew four. Their goals for were 74, goals against 15 – and, as previously mentioned, their Cup win was achieved with a totally clean sheet. The team was predominantly Scottish, England centre-forward John Goodall the star 'foreigner'.

Preston also won the League the following year, despite four defeats, with Everton second – a foretaste of things to come, since the positions were reversed in the 1890-91 season. Preston claimed runners-up spot for three seasons running, underlining their claim to be the first major force in League football. That last season saw the 12 founder members become 14 with the addition of Stoke and Darwen.

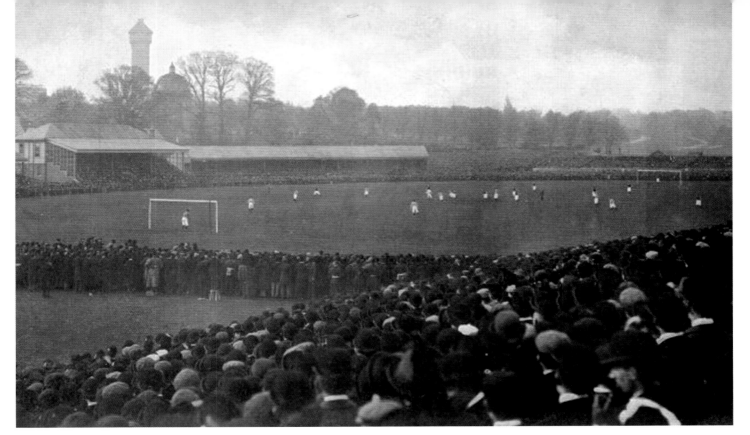

The original intention was that League points should be awarded solely for wins. But after 10 weeks of the first season, this was amended to make drawn games yield one point apiece as compared to two for a win – a system that remained in operation until 1981-82, when the proliferation of goalless draws encouraged the League to improve the points for a win to three.

'Proud' Preston's mantle was donned in the 1890s by Sunderland, who took the League title in the seasons 1891-92,1892-93 and again in 1894-95, having finished second to Aston Villa in the intervening season. Their success stoked the fires of football fervour in the Northeast, where the industrial base provided by shipbuilding supplied both the men to play football and the crowds to watch.

The team also included a Scots contingent, drawn southwards across the border in search of fame and fortune. One of these, goalkeeper Ned Doig, played against West Bromwich on 20 September 1890 before his transfer from Arbroath had been formally registered, costing his new club two points. He proved a worthwhile buy in the long term, however. In seven seasons, the team were beaten only once at Roker Park. Sunderland were known as the 'Team of All the Talents'.

In 1892-93, their first Championship campaign, they topped 100 goals for the first time in League history, being assisted by the expansion of the division to 16 clubs. This feat was not to be equalled until the interwar years when West Bromwich notched 104 goals in a 22-club division. Sunderland had not, in fact, been one of the founding 12, but their history was impressive enough. Added to the League strength in 1890 when Stoke temporarily dropped out, they retained their First Division place until 1958. By then, they had added another three Championships to their 1890s successes.

Aston Villa from the Midlands had been first to challenge northern supremacy. As previously noted, they won in 1893-94, and were from 1895-96 to monopolise the title for the five seasons to the end of the century, save a single win (in 1897-98) by Sheffield United. The latter had joined the League in 1893, a year after their city rivals Wednesday.

The League had added a 12-strong Second Division for the season 1892-93, simultaneously adding a further two teams to the First. The lower echelon had previously been known as the Football Alliance, a competition set up in 1889 by a group of non-League teams which had shown its collective class by drawing in a representative match with a League XI. The promotion and relegation issues were to be settled by a series of three test matches, these pitting Second Division champions against the bottom First Division club, runners-up against second

• **Above**
Aston Villa contested the 1897 FA Cup Final against Everton, running out 3-2 winners.

from bottom and third-placed against the third from bottom. As a result Sheffield United and Darwen were promoted, with Notts County – one of the founding 12 – relegated.

This arrangement was, of course, all but duplicated in the 1980s when play-offs were introduced, initially with the purpose of reducing the size of the First Division but subsequently retained to add excitement to the end-of-season action. In 1892-93, however, Birmingham Small Heath could consider themselves unlucky in having topped the lower division yet missing out on promotion, there being then no automatic place.

The system was dispensed with after an 1898 fixture between Stoke and Burnley which ended in a goalless draw – coincidentally or otherwise, a result that kept both clubs in the top flight. Thereafter, an automatic two up/two down system of promotion and relegation was instituted. This was modified to three-up, three-down in 1973-74, the third place being made the subject of a play-off in 1986-87. The new division had failed to admit a single club from the south: that had to wait until the election of Woolwich Arsenal to the Second Division in 1893. By 1894-95 there were 16 clubs in each division.

The League and Cup Double has remained a cherished dream for First Division clubs: only one team managed to repeat Preston's inaugural feat before the end of the century. Aston Villa achieved the distinction in 1897 as part of the four Championships in five seasons that rounded off the decade and indeed the century. The magnitude of their feat is underlined by the fact that the runners-up Sheffield United trailed a full 11 points behind.

No-one would emulate their achievement for fully 64 years until the Spurs team of 1960-61 recorded the first Double of the modern era.

Securing the League title some while before the end of the season must have helped, but the ease of Villa's first-round despatch of Newcastle United, 5-0, was not matched by their third-round jitters against Preston. No longer quite the force they were, North End nevertheless took Villa to a third game before succumbing by the narrowest of 3-2 margins. Up until the replay, Villa had profited from home advantage throughout the Cup.

Beating Liverpool with ease 3-0 in the semi-final, Villa faced their Merseyside rivals at Crystal Palace, defeating them 3-2 to add the Cup to the prize already secured. One of the powerhouses of this team was half-back John Reynolds, an international for both England and Ireland (though born in Blackburn). Villa had won the Cup two years earlier, defeating West Bromwich by a single goal at the first Crystal Palace final. The Cup won in Double year was a different one since, after lending it to sports outfitter William Shillcock for display in his window, they never saw it again. The £25 which Villa were fined for this misdemeanour paid for a new trophy. A newspaper interview with an 83-year-old, Harry Burge, in 1958 claimed the Cup was melted down to manufacture forged coin.

The FA Cup provided surprises in the following two years. In 1900, non-League Southampton battled to the final before being dispatched in no uncertain fashion, 4-0, by Bury of the First Division. The following year, however, saw even more of a shock when Tottenham Hotspur became the first – and still

the only – non-League club to win the Cup since 1888. They took two games to defeat Sheffield United, runners-up in the League the season before but 14th out of 18th that year despite the stopping skills of legendary 21-stone goalkeeper 'Fatty' Foulke.

A replay at Burnden Park, Bolton, was required to settle matters 3-1 after a 2-2 draw at Crystal Palace. Centre-forward Sandy Brown also set a record by scoring in every round of the competition – a record total of 15 goals that has yet to be surpassed. He notched three of these in the finals, including both Spurs' strikes in the original game. Spurs were then members of the Southern League and remained outside the Football League until 1908: their first season in the Second Division saw them finish second and obtain promotion. Interestingly, their Cup-winning team had contained 11 Northerners.

One of the main reasons the game of football took off in Scotland in preference to rugby may well be the fact that well-grassed areas were few and far between, especially in the Scottish lowlands. Soccer could be – and frequently was – improvised anywhere and everywhere. On 9 July 1867 the Queen's Park Football Club was founded in Glasgow, where there were only three parks to alleviate the need to play on cobbles.

The club was founded at 3 Eglinton Terrace, Glasgow, three brothers named Smith being among those present. One, Robert, was soon to be appointed Scotland's first national captain. Those he consorted with on this occasion included soccer enthusiasts, YMCA members and a number of Highland Games specialists who all used the park whose name they adopted. First games were strictly intramural, the members splitting into north and south of the River Clyde. As the game grew in popularity elsewhere, competitive games were introduced, the first of these being in August 1868 against a club named Thistle.

Over the three years following their formation, Queen's Park were to attract Scotland's best players to their ranks, dominating the Scottish scene. The establishment of international matches with England broadened their horizons and they soon joined the FA to take part in the first FA Cup competitions. As recorded earlier, they did so with some success, reaching two Finals before the newly-formed Scottish Football Association outlawed their participation in 1887. Their opponents in each case were Blackburn Rovers, the scores 2-1 and 2-0.

Queen's Park's total dominance of football north of the border can be gauged by the fact that all but two of the team that met England in the first international on Scottish soil on 30 November 1872 were from the club. The two exceptions, two of the Smith brothers, were both ex-members now living in London. The gate receipts from the match, a goalless draw, were £200, with the 4,000 spectators each charged one shilling admission. Such untold riches

• **Above**
Spurs and Sheffield United play out a 2-2 draw in the 1901 Cup Final at Crystal Palace.

encouraged Queen's Park to seek larger accommodation, which became available in the shape of Hampden Park. This is still the home of Queen's Park FC and the venue at which Scotland's international matches are played.

It was obvious that forming a Scottish equivalent to the English FA would stimulate competition for places in the national side, while playing teams nearer home would make life a lot easier for Queen's Park. If proof were needed, one only had to recall that in 1872 and 1873, the first two years of the FA Cup, the Scots had been obliged to scratch at the semi-final stage (the first time after forcing a draw) through lack of funds.

Thus it was that 1873 saw the formation of the eight-team Scottish FA. Seven founder members agreed to accept the rules by which Queen's Park played, since the Glasgow club had always believed itself superior to all other Scots teams of whatever level. Of those eight founder members, only Queen's Park and Kilmarnock survive today: the others, for the record, were Clydesdale, Vale of Leven, Third Lanark, Dumbreck, Eastern and Granville.

Such was Queen's Park's continuing superiority that it was not until 16 January 1875 that an opponent even managed to score against them, the team in question being Vale of Leven. Elsewhere, standards were equally uneven: the legendary 36-0 win by Arbroath against Bon Accord in 1885 still stands as the record British first-class football score.

As with Queen's Park, the clubs affiliated to the Scottish FA could, in the early years, compete against English clubs or even be members of both English and Scottish bodies. This was, however, soon

to change, the catalyst being the advent of professionalism in England. The Scottish FA chose to bar 68 Scots playing south of the border, regarding professionalism as 'evil'. Queen's Park, who today remain the only Scottish League club to have amateur status, were in the forefront of this crusade. Clashes in the 1886-87 FA Cup exacerbated the situation, and Rangers, who went out to Aston Villa in the semi-final held at Crewe, were to be the last Scottish club to venture south.

International matches, of course, continued, with Scotland having by far the upper hand, notching seven wins and two draws in the 11 fixtures since that first Glasgow game. This dominance owed much to Queen's Park's players reproducing club form for their country – as indeed one would expect when the players concerned made up the majority of the team. England selected mainly from top amateur club the Corinthians, ensuring that the taint of professionalism was not felt in this fixture for some time.

The SFA edict that clubs should not belong to any other national organisation nor compete in their competitions meant a Scottish League was desperately needed. Such a body was formed in 1890 and was, as one would expect, initially proudly amateur. Dumbarton and Rangers shared the first Championship, drawing in a play-off game – the only such occasion in the history of the League. Dumbarton emerged to take the title outright the following season.

The inevitable quickening of the southwards migration from the all-amateur Scottish game by the most gifted players led to another rash of expulsions.

The annual internationals were proving something of a headache, however, since Scotland refused to pick the 'exiles' and inevitably suffered for their pains at the hands of the British professionals. A 5-2 drubbing in 1893 at Richmond was the turning point – and when Celtic, that year's champions, moved a motion to accept professionalism in the Scottish League the old guard was routed.

Queen's Park, who had not joined the League, found it impossible to maintain their leading position on an amateur basis. Although they beat champions Celtic to take the 1893 Scottish Cup, it was a pyrrhic victory, and despite swallowing their pride and joining the League in 1899 they were never to scale such heights again. They remain amateurs to this day.

The 1893 team to play England was divided 5-4 between Queen's Park – the team of the past – and Celtic, one of the two teams of the future. Even though the Scottish League grew swiftly – after its first season it could claim the affiliation of 64 clubs in associated leagues – it was thenceforth to be dominated by the two Glasgow clubs, Rangers and Celtic.

The 'Old Firm', as they became known, carved up the championship to such an extent that their domination was broken only 13 times by outside clubs between the advent of professionalism in 1893-94 and the introduction of a new three-division system in 1974. (There are currently a Premier League and three lower divisions.) A Second Division was established in 1893, although promotion and relegation between the two divisions was far from automatic. This was not to be resolved until these teams, disenchanted by the old boys network, withdrew to form an unrecognised Central League.

Back in England, the venue of the FA Cup Final had settled at Crystal Palace in 1895, having moved northwards from the Oval, with its limited 25,000 capacity, to Fallowfield, Manchester in 1893. This arrangement proved disastrous, and Goodison Park, Merseyside was a more successful venue in 1894 before a permanent home for the fixture was found at Crystal Palace. Crowds approached 100,000, a figure achieved in 1905 when Aston Villa beat Newcastle United in the latter's first Double attempt. This was only the second time a match had attracted this figure, the first being 1901 when 114,815 attended. The Football Association introduced extra time in 1913 as a method to decide the destination of the Cup at the first attempt: it proved effective, replays proving unnecessary until 1970. But the FA Cup Final would reside at the Palace only until the outbreak of World War I.

Newcastle United, feeding off the north-east hotbed of football fervour, dominated the upper reaches of the Football League at this time, yet though their achievements were noteworthy they couldn't quite follow through. They first stood on the threshold of the League and Cup Double in 1905, but a 0-2 Cup Final reverse against Aston Villa dashed their hopes of adding it to the League Championship. In 1906 they could only finish fourth, running up in the Cup again to Everton. In 1907 came another Championship win, though an early Cup defeat against non-League opposition proved

• Above
The presentation of the 1911 FA Cup to Bradford City at Old Trafford, after their 1-0 defeat of Newcastle.

hard to swallow. 1908 saw a repeat of 1906, losing 3-1 to Wolves. The League followed the year after and in 1910 they finally won the Cup.

Victory over Barnsley by 2-0 at Goodison Park after a 1-1 draw at Crystal Palace seemed to confirm the popular theory that they found it hard to compete away from their own St James's Park – Crystal Palace's lush turf being one reason put forward. In 1911 the form book proved true again, when they lost to Bradford City after a replay. By not losing first time they could claim to be improving! With five Cup Finals and three Championships in seven seasons, they could consider themselves unlucky not to have done the Double.

Their playmaker was Scots half-back Peter McWilliam, while the cunning defensive play of Irishman Billy McCracken and his defensive partner Hudspeth is covered elsewhere in discussion of the offside rule they used so often to their advantage. So parsimonious was their defence, however, that their 1909 League win had been secured with just 65 'goals for', thanks to a miserly total of 41 against.

Aston Villa had taken two League Championships at the end of the decade (and century), but apart from Sheffield Wednesday's consecutive League wins in 1902-03 and 1903-04, the title changed hands with surprising regularity. Oldham nearly capped their brief period in the top flight with a Championship win, losing out in the final game of the 1914-15 season, the last before war halted competition.

Another Lancashire team, Blackburn, was more successful, winning two Championships in 1912 and 1914 and filling homely Ewood Park more weeks than not. Their captain was the influential Bob Crompton. Manchester United won Championships in 1908 and 1911. 1909 nearly saw the League suspended due to a players' strike in favour of the Football Players and Trainers Union, evidence of the working-class backgrounds from which most of the players now emerged. Despite this effective show of solidarity, it was to be 50 years and more before a player challenged the concept of a maximum wage, decided upon as far back as 1901.

The First Golden Age

CHAPTER TWO

2

The First Golden Age

The catalyst for the rapid development of football as the national game was the formation of the Football League in 1888. It was not so much the more structured arrangements that were important, rather it was the fillip the League gave to the professional game. Amateur sides with intriguing names like the Wanderers, Royal Engineers and Clapham Rovers had dominated both the early years of the FA Cup and the make-up of the England national side, traditionally drawn from Old Carthusians, Oxford University and Corinthians, the outstanding amateur clubs of the era.

It was, however, the professional footballer playing for northern clubs who would dominate the new competition. And this would be the hallmark of English football in the first decades of the twentieth-century. Of the 12 original League members, half were from Lancashire and five from the Midlands, together with Stoke from Staffordshire.

Even when the First Division was extended to 16 teams and a 12-club Second Division was introduced in 1892, none of the 28 was from further south than Birmingham. They took over the FA Cup and national side as well. Northern and Midlands clubs provided both FA Cup finalists every year from 1888 until Southern League Southampton were beaten by Bury in the 1900 Final. From 1890 onwards, moreover, the selection of amateurs for England was the exception rather than the norm.

The south-east of England, for so long a stronghold of the amateur game, was slow off the professional mark, but was starting to catch up as the twentieth-century got under way. In 1901, Spurs became the first London professional side (and the last non-League club) to win the Cup. By then, Arsenal were playing in the Second Division, the first of five clubs from the capital in the two divisions of the League by 1908.

Outside the Football League, moreover, the Southern League was in effect the Edwardian equivalent of the Third Division. As the name implies, it comprised clubs from the south-east and, after seeing its top clubs elected occasionally to the Football League before the First World War, the Southern League First Division became the Third Division when the Football League was extended in 1919.

The growing interest from the urban working classes meant football had to be more professional in all aspects of its organisation. Attendances rose rapidly. The best estimates of Everton's home gates, for example, suggest an average of 7,260 in the first League season. Just ten years later, it was up to

17,390 and by the last season before the Great War, 1913-14, the average was up to 25,250. Other clubs showed similar trends. Aston Villa and Bolton both went from around 4,500 a game in 1888-89 to 25,000 by 1913-14.

In the final three peacetime seasons, Chelsea were the best-supported club in the country and, in 1913-14, their average gate topped 37,000. The 1901 FA Cup Final between Spurs and Sheffield United at the old Crystal Palace ground attracted the first recorded six-figure attendance, officially shown as 114,815. This was topped when Aston Villa and Sunderland met at the same ground for the 1913 Final. The attendance that day was recorded as 120,081, a 60-fold increase on the 2,000 crowd which had witnessed the first FA Cup Final at Kennington Oval in 1872.

The professional game in the years up to 1914 was very much 'the People's Game'. It was cheap and simple and the improvements in public transport made it more accessible. The urban working environment was crucial to its development, providing not only supporters but also players, club owners and directors.

• Opposite and above
The legendary 1923 'White Horse' FA Cup Final between West Ham and Bolton, the first to be held at Wembley Stadium.

Blackburn Grammar School (Blackburn Rovers), Wyggeston School (Leicester City) and Droop Street School (QPR).

To accommodate growing crowds, clubs had to provide better facilities. More was invested in new grounds in this era than at any time before the publication of the Taylor Report led to a surge of new building work in the 1990s. The most famous architect of football stadiums in the early years of the twentieth century was Archibald Leitch. His work could be seen to best effect at in the original structures at Fulham's Craven Cottage, Blackburn's Ewood Park, Everton's Goodison Park and the Dell in Southampton.

Other aspects of professionalism began to emerge. Although televised football is a relatively recent phenomenon, newspapers quickly recognised the value of football coverage. In fact, there was enough interest to sustain a weekly

Many businessmen, recognising the interest their workers had in football, started to participate in the development of local clubs. Similarly, workers from particular companies formed football teams which subsequently became Stoke, Manchester United and Arsenal. The church was also an important influence in the early days of clubs like Aston Villa, Bolton, Everton and Fulham, as were schools such as

newspaper, the *Athletic News*, devoted almost entirely to football. Published in Manchester every Monday, it contained full reports and line-ups for every first-class game, including the Southern League. To promote sales, cigarette companies in the Edwardian era introduced sets of cards with a football theme, which today command remarkable prices.

• Above
John Devey in action for Aston Villa, the outstanding pre-war team.

Industrial unrest and scandals were also part and parcel of the emerging professional game. Financial scandals were ten a penny and generally came in two flavours. The first, at a time when attendances were rising and the game becoming more popular but the players were paid a maximum of £4 a week, took the form of illegal payments. Although seven clubs were investigated for financial irregularities at this time (QPR, Sunderland, Manchester City and United, Glossop, Coventry and Middlesbrough) many more were thought to have been in breach of the rules.

The biggest name caught in the net was Manchester City, FA Cup winners in 1904, and among those to pay the penalty of a year's suspension was Billy Meredith, the biggest star of the day who had scored the winning goal in the Final. He was unrepentant, and his outspoken manner did not help his case. Not only were payments over and above the maximum wage involved, players often asked for more than the standard £10 signing-on fee when they moved clubs. Many got it, but those who were reported for asking paid a heavy price.

• Above
Billy Meredith (left), a gifted but controversial figure.

• Inset
Joe Bache, who played 474 times for Aston Villa between 1900-20, scoring 184 goals.

33

• Above
Burnley's disgraced goalkeeper Jack Hillman, convicted of taking bribes.

The second type of financial scandal was attempting to fix matches. Jack Hillman, Burnley's international goalkeeper, was found guilty of trying to bribe a Nottingham Forest player before a vital relegation game in 1900 (which Forest won). This was not the only instance of the misdemeanour but it was the most high-profile. It showed the increasing pressures on clubs in a professional era to play at the highest level and win trophies.

At a time when the game appeared to be booming, professional sportsmen were having their pay controlled by directors and administrators who knew little about football. The resentment this bred gave legitimacy to the first attempts at forming a players union. In this respect, footballers were no different from many other industrial groups who were using collective action in Asquith's Liberal England to voice their discontent – but the relationship between the clubs and the union reflected the worst sort of master-servant industrial partnership. Only the threat of strike action by the players in 1909-10 persuaded the club chairmen to recognise the union, but the maximum wage remained (until the 1960s) and the leading union activists, even star names such as Manchester United's Charlie Roberts and Billy Meredith, were thought to have been 'victimised'.

More evidence of the growing commercialisation of football came with the development of the transfer market. Players moved frequently, and usually at the club's rather than the player's behest. Transfer fees were modest but grew in the early years of the twentieth century until the sensational transfer of Alf Common from Sunderland to Middlesbrough for £1,000 in 1905, the first-ever four-figure fee. This led to attempts to limit transfer fees but ever-inventive clubs soon found ways around the rules. The most obvious was to sell two players for the maximum combined fee, one of whom was only a makeweight. By January 1913, the £2,000 ceiling was breached for the first time when non-League West Ham sold Danny Shea to Blackburn Rovers.

On the field, the game was slower, more deliberate and more physical than today. Levels of physical fitness were much lower then than now and training comprised road runs and a few exercises. Coaching was almost unknown and many clubs believed in 'starving' the players of the ball until the match on Saturdays. Under the old offside law, the centre-half was an auxiliary attacker but the goal count was generally low, full-backs like Morley and Montgomery at Notts County and McCracken at Newcastle having learnt how to exploit the offside trap to stifle opponents' attacking play.

With chairmen more important in matters of team selection than managers, tactics were left pretty much to the players to work out for themselves and, as far as they existed, they were very basic. Most clubs adopted a 2-3-5 formation with wing-halves and inside-forwards performing the modern midfield roles. With most clubs using two wingers, the ball

was worked in triangles down both flanks before crossing to a large, physically intimidating centre forward. Football was then a passing game, generally credited to the Scottish influence, ball control and dribbling the prized skills.

Throughout this period, there were only two major domestic competitions, the Football League and the FA Cup. The Football League Cup was not introduced until 1960-61, five years after the first season of European club competition.

Football was more 'democratic' in these early years, with the honours spread more evenly around the clubs. In the 27 seasons between 1888 and 1915, there were 54 trophies at stake, which were won by 20 different clubs, as follows:

• Above
Alf Common, whose transfer from Sunderland to Middlesbrough in 1905 attracted the first four-figure fee in football.

No. of Wins	Football Club
10	Aston Villa
5	Sunderland
4	Newcastle, The Wednesday, Sheffield United and Blackburn Rovers
3	Preston, Everton and Manchester United
2	Liverpool, Wolverhampton Wanderers and Bury
1	West Bromwich Albion, Notts County, Nottingham Forest, Tottenham Hotspur, Manchester City, Bradford City, Barnsley and Burnley

The most consistently successful club over the period from the formation of the Football League to the outbreak of the Great War was Aston Villa. They had several outstanding teams and won ten trophies and finished runners-up six times in 22 seasons. On six occasions, the League title went to Villa Park, including five times in seven years between 1893 and 1900.

In that same decade were two FA Cup successes, including 1896-97, a year they also won the League, and this was to be the last Double until Spurs in 1960-61. The League was won again in 1909-10 and Villa were runners-up five times in these years. The FA Cup Final of 1913 was between the two top teams in the (old) First Division. On the day of the Final, the fate of the Championship was still to be decided and either club could have done the Double. Villa took the Cup but missed out on ` the League.

The great names from those days are now long-forgotten to all but historians and collectors of cigarette cards. Crabtree, Devey, Spencer and Cowan were names to conjure with in the 1890s and, after the turn of the century, those of Hampton, Bache, Ducat and Hardy were no less illustrious. It was all achieved without a manager but the contribution of secretary George Ramsey should be recognised.

The English game was very inward looking at this time, and would remain so until after the Second World War. This was partly because British football was more advanced in technical and organisational terms than in Europe, and partly because international travel was much more primitive. (Ironically, it would be English coaches, like Jimmy Hogan who, either side of the Great War, helped the European game to develop to the point where it was at least the equal of the English.) An insular mentality may also have been a contributory factor.

The Home International Championship was the major international tournament, the clash between England and Scotland the main game. There was also the occasional close season tour of Europe. For players like Bob Crompton, therefore, to win 41 caps implied an international career that stretched over a dozen or so seasons. Confidence that all was well with English football at international level came with success in the 1908 and 1912 Olympic Games, when the gold medal for football was twice won comfortably by British teams. But the apparent superiority of the English game proved to be illusory.

Though Sunderland had been the north-east's powerhouse of football in the first years of the Football League, the early years of the twentieth century saw the Wearsiders eclipsed by their neighbours on the Tyne. Newcastle went on to set standards in the Edwardian era few clubs have since matched. After several years of challenging, the Magpies made the breakthrough in 1904-05. Not only was the League title won in style but they also came close to the elusive Double, losing to Aston Villa in front of over 120,000 people in the FA Cup Final at Crystal Palace. In each of the next six seasons, however, Newcastle were either League champions or FA Cup finalists.

There were two (old) First Division titles (1906-07 and 1908-09) and Cup Final appearances in 1906, 1908, 1910 and 1911. Strangely, the Magpies could never win at Crystal Palace. Their only FA Cup success was in 1910 when, after a draw in London, they beat Barnsley at Goodison Park.

The team was filled with some of the big names

• **Opposite**
Early FA Cup action. The competition was won by 16 different clubs between the wars.

• **Above**
Bob Crompton (left) steered Blackburn to League titles in 1912 and 1914, as well as winning 41 caps for England.

of the day, only a few of whom are remembered today – the likes of Billy McCracken, whose tactical nous contributed to a change in the offside law 20 years later, the elegant Peter McWilliam, who later found further fame as a manager with Spurs, the multi-talented Colin Veitch and long-serving goalkeeper Jimmy Lawrence. In charge was a secretary, Frank Watt, rather than a manager, who was shrewd enough to let a group of supremely gifted individuals play the game their way.

The inter-war period was something of a contradiction for English football. The Football League and FA Cup competitions were even more popular than in the pre-1914 period, a critical change in the laws tried to make the game more open and attacking, and a national stadium was acquired. More worrying, however, was the fact that the insularity of the English game was becoming exposed. Not only did the FA decline to take part in either of the first two World Cup competitions, but the technical frailties of the England team at international level were also starting to become apparent.

Immediately on the resumption of the League programme in 1919, a third division was created out of the Southern League. A fourth division followed 12 months later, the two new divisions becoming the Third South and Third North. Only the champions were promoted to Division Two and the bottom clubs were subject to re-election at the League's AGM each year rather than to automatic demotion.

Thus, the 12-club, one-division League of 1888 had grown to two divisions and 40 clubs by 1914. By the second inter-war season there were 88 clubs competing in four equal-size divisions, which is how it remained through to 1939. Professional League football was in effect extended to all parts of England and Wales, becoming a truly national game.

The inter-war League campaigns were dominated by two clubs, Huddersfield in the 1920s and Arsenal in the 1930s. Both clubs managed hat-tricks of League titles, and were also runners-up on other occasions, the first signs that the First Division title was becoming a private competition between a relatively small number of clubs. In the 20 inter-war seasons, there were just ten different winners of the League Championship, five of whom won it on more than one occasion.

The FA Cup, on the other hand, was won by 16

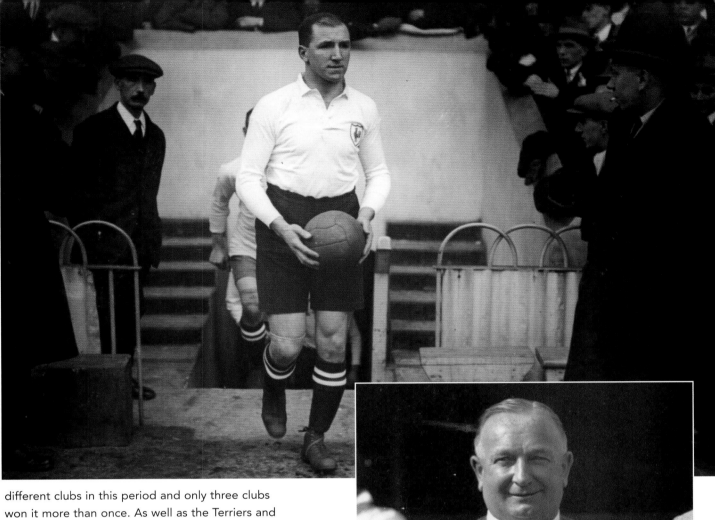

different clubs in this period and only three clubs won it more than once. As well as the Terriers and the Gunners, six clubs (Newcastle, West Brom, Everton, Manchester City, Sheffield Wednesday and Sunderland) won both competitions in these years.

Huddersfield Town had risen without trace to become the major power in English football in the decade immediately following the First World War. Yet only two months into the new era, in November 1919, Huddersfield were faced by a financial crisis that threatened them with a transfer to nearby Leeds, whose club had been expelled from the League the previous month for financial irregularities. Local support saved the club which, remarkably, went on to win promotion from the Second Division that season and to make the FA Cup Final, only to lose to Aston Villa at Stamford Bridge. From these turbulent beginnings, the Terriers soared to new heights.

The appointment of Herbert Chapman as manager in March 1921 was a turning point. The FA Cup was won the following month when Preston were beaten by a penalty, and the League Championship went to Leeds Road in three consecutive seasons between 1923 and 1926. By the time the hat-trick was completed, Chapman had

been enticed to Arsenal, but the team was good enough to survive his departure. In 1926-27, Huddersfield were runners-up in the League, and 12 months later they again finished second and lost at Wembley to Blackburn. Under manager Clem

• **Above**
Arthur Grimsdell captained Tottenham Hotspur to the 1921 FA Cup in one of the last pre-Wembley Finals held at Stamford Bridge.

• **Inset**
Herbert Chapman was the period's most successful and influential manager.

Stephenson, one of the stars of Chapman's Huddersfield, the club had two more losing Wembley appearances in the interwar period, to Arsenal in 1930 and ironically, to Preston in 1938, by a penalty.

Chapman's new club, Arsenal, dominated the 1930s to an extent only Liverpool in the 1980s and Manchester United in the 1990s have since matched. The first signs of stirring in North London came in 1927, when the Gunners reached their first FA Cup Final, only to lose to the softest of goals.

This was the team that Herbert Chapman built, bankrolled initially by the club's controversial chairman, Sir Henry Norris, and it got better. He bought big, with the likes of Alex James and David Jack and, more modestly, paying relatively small sums for such outstanding players as Eddie Hapgood, Cliff Bastin and Joe Hulme.

The first honour was won in 1930, when Arsenal defeated Chapman's former club Huddersfield 2-0 to lift the FA Cup at Wembley. The victory marked the ending of the 1920s and the start of the 1930s in more senses than one. The first Football League Championship followed 12 months later, with 66 points, a new record. A near Double in 1931-32, runners-up in both League and Cup, was followed by a hat-trick of League titles.

Half-way through this sequence, Chapman died, but it was business as usual under his successor, BBC commentator George Allison, whose first signing was Ted Drake. A fifth Championship was unexpectedly won in 1937-38, with just 52 points, the lowest for a side finishing top in a 42-match campaign, but not before a second Wembley triumph, against Sheffield United

in 1936.

Yet the First Division was still more open than the Premiership is today. During the 1920s and 1930s, only three clubs, Arsenal, Liverpool and Sunderland, had unbroken membership of the top flight. And fortunes could turn very quickly. Everton, champions in 1928, finished bottom of the table two years later. The Toffees, however, bounced straight back as Second Division champions in 1930-31 and remarkably reclaimed the League title the following year. Manchester City, champions in 1936-37, were relegated 12 months later, despite being the First Division's highest scorers. West Brom, Burnley, Newcastle and Sheffield Wednesday, champions during the 1920s, all suffered the indignity of relegation a few years later.

The Cup provided much of the footballing glamour of the period. For the first three post-Great War seasons, however, the FA Cup was virtually homeless, using Chelsea's Stamford Bridge to stage the Final. Then, in 1923, Wembley played host for the first time. Built for the Empire Exhibition, it was acquired by Arthur Elvin and used for all Cup finals and most of England's Home Internationals until 2000. (It was also used for speedway, rugby league,

the 1948 Olympics and even for show jumping.)

By the end of the twentieth century, however, Wembley was tired and the facilities compared unfavourably with many modern club grounds. But those flickering cinematic images of the first game, the 1923 FA Cup Final between Bolton and West Ham, are among the most immediately recognisable of football scenes. An official crowd of 126,000 saw some of the match, which Bolton won 2-0, although unofficial estimates put the real figure closer to 200,000.

The elegant David Jack scored Wembley's first goal which helped Bolton to the first of three FA Cup victories in six years, achieved without conceding a goal in any Final. It was the first of many memorable Cup moments associated with the new stadium. Upsets are the essence of Cup football and Cardiff's victory over Arsenal in 1927 (by a soft goal conceded by Welsh keeper Dan Lewis) and Blackburn's 1928 triumph over the then mighty Huddersfield were among the biggest surprises. In 1931, West Brom completed a double of sorts, winning the Cup and promotion from Division Two in the same season.

The following year saw one of Wembley's most controversial moments when Newcastle's Allen

• **Opposite**
Centre-forward Ted Drake, whose seven-goal game for Arsenal against Villa in 1935 cemented a place in legend.

• **Above**
The Huddersfield Town side, which, managed by Herbert Chapman (left, back row) won three League titles.

41

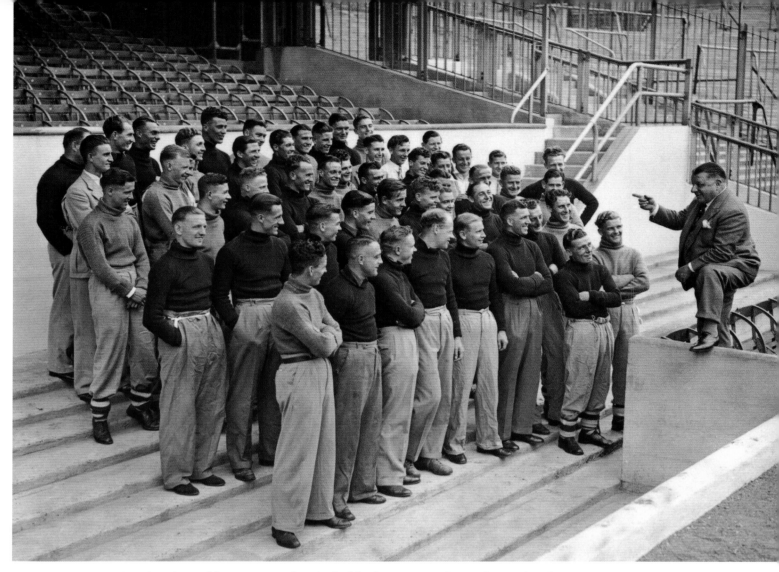

• **Above**
Arsenal receive a pep talk from manager George Allison.

scored against Arsenal from a cross after the ball had clearly crossed the by-line. The teenage Frank Swift fainting at the final whistle in 1934, the drama of Sheffield Wednesday's two late, late goals against West Brom in 1935, the tension of George Mutch's last-minute penalty for Preston against Huddersfield in 1938 and finally Jack Tinn's spats and Portsmouth's unlikely triumph over Wolves in the last peacetime Final are all enduring parts of Wembley legend.

The Huddersfield and Arsenal sides which both won a hat-trick of League titles were not only linked by their management, but exemplified much that was happening in English football at the time. Herbert Chapman not only put both clubs on the footballing map but defined the job of football manager in a way that the modern supporter would understand.

Until Chapman, managers were largely administrators, the link between the board and the players. But to the players, many managers were remote figures with little involvement in tactics or even team selection, a prerogative many chairman were reluctant to relinquish. Much was left to the trainers, who took responsibility for fitness, while playing formations were often left to the players to work out.

Chapman changed this and a lot more besides, taking charge of all aspects of club affairs. He was tactically adroit and spotted opportunities when the offside law was modified, he made more imaginative and bolder use of the transfer market than his peers, he handled star players as individuals and coaxed improved performances out of them. He was acutely aware of the value of publicity and he was a strict disciplinarian who demanded total loyalty and the highest standards of behaviour from his players. He was also a visionary on issues such as floodlights, his thinking far in advance of the football authorities. And he was successful.

Yet there was little in his early career to suggest that he was going to rewrite the record books. A journeyman player with Grimsby, Swindon, Northampton, Sheffield United, Notts County and Tottenham, he stumbled into management with Southern League Northampton when a Spurs colleague turned it down and suggested Chapman go for it. Within two years, he had taken the Cobblers to their divisional title and in 1912 he was on his way back to his native Yorkshire to manage Second Division Leeds City. His career nearly foundered when he was implicated (and suspended) in the financial scandal than led to Leeds City being wound up. But then nearby Huddersfield gave him a chance to resurrect his career, first as assistant manager and then, from March 1921, as manager. He wasted no time proving his worth.

Chapman was lucky with his inheritance. Huddersfield had been promoted from Division Two and reached the FA Cup Final (losing to Aston Villa) in 1920, just before he succeeded Ambrose Langley. In his first full season, the new manager took the Terriers to another Stamford Bridge final, which this time they won, beating Preston 1-0, the club and manager's first major honour. This was only the springboard for greater success. In 1923-24, the League Championship went to Leeds Road by the narrowest of margins. Had Cardiff's Len Davies scored from a penalty in the final match against Birmingham, the title would have gone to Wales. It stayed in Yorkshire for the next two seasons but, by then, Chapman was in London.

Sir Henry Norris, the flamboyant (and ultimately corrupt) chairman of Arsenal had persuaded Chapman to move south in the 1925 close season. Chapman relished the bigger stage that the capital offered and his first major move showed his original thinking. He signed Sunderland's outstanding but ageing inside-forward Charlie Buchan. Arsenal's offer for the 34-year-old fell well below the Wearsiders asking price and Chapman's novel solution was to agree a modest £2,000 fee and £100 for every goal he scored in his first season. In the end, Buchan cost Arsenal £4,100, and both sides were happy.

In 1928, Chapman broke the rules again when he paid the first £10,000 fee to Bolton for the gifted David Jack, in effect Buchan's replacement. By then, other bits of his jigsaw were falling into place and, with the signings of Alex James, Cliff Bastin and Eddie Hapgood, the team that was to dominate the 1930s was coming together.

It was not just a question of the players, however. Chapman was the first to figure out the tactical implications of a change in the offside law. In 1925, to encourage more attacking play, the authorities reduced the number of defenders that had to be between the foremost attacker and the goal from three to two. The immediate results were

• **Above**
287 goals in 547 first-class appearances made Arsenal and England's David Jack the first £10,000 footballer.

encouraging. In the last season under the old rule, 1924-25, 1,182 goals were scored in the First Division. The following year, the total soared by 43% to 1,703, up from an average of 2.6 to 3.7 goals per game.

What Chapman quickly realised, however, is that defensive strategies had to change. Where previously the centre-half was almost an extra attacker, the new rule led to the centre-half becoming a 'stopper' or 'third back' and in Herbie Roberts he had the ideal exponent of the new role. It encouraged counter-attacking play, the swift break, with a ball out of defence to James in midfield and then on to wingers Hulme or Bastin to attack down the flanks or cut in to score. A consistent feature of Chapman's teams were the goals scored by the wide men.

The honours went to Highbury thick and fast, five League titles and three Cup Final appearances in nine seasons. In 1931-32, one of only two trophyless seasons in this period, they came close to doing the Double but won nothing largely because of an injury to James in the closing weeks of the campaign and a dreadful refereeing decision at Wembley against

Newcastle, the 'over-the-line' Final. Chapman missed out on the completion of the hat-trick. He died, aged 55, after catching a cold watching a non-League game at Guildford.

The tag 'Lucky Arsenal' was soon applied to Chapman's Gunners but the results and the crowds tell a different story. For nine consecutive seasons from 1929-30, Arsenal were the most consistent side and the best-supported club in country. Based on the official Football League statistics, it appears the average gate at Highbury climbed from 29,845 the season before he arrived to a peak of 46,252 in the hat-trick season of 1934-35.

Chapman's legacy was immense, and it touched so many different areas. To travellers on the London Underground, for example, he bequeathed a station when Gillespie Road on the Piccadilly Line became Highbury at his urging. The facilities at the Highbury ground were considerably improved and, from his North London base, he created not only a team and a club but also a role that set the standards for his successors. Chairmen were still key figures at clubs, but, post-Chapman, managers were increasingly in the spotlight on all team-related matters.

And in one other respect, he could see clearly the future direction of football. In 1934, Arsenal provided seven of the England team which beat World Champions Italy in what became known as 'the Battle of Highbury'. Chapman was also in charge of a national squad that made a close-season tour of Europe and he saw at first hand what was happening in football outside the United Kingdom. He was fearful English football would get left behind by the technical advances made in Europe some 20 years before the Hungarians gave the English a football lesson at Wembley.

Through the work of English coaches like Jimmy Hogan, continental football had made great strides, although the English public was quite unaware of these developments. Between 1919 and 1929, the English national side played exactly 50 internationals, two-thirds of which were in the Home International Championship against Ireland, Scotland or Wales. The only 'overseas' countries played were Belgium, France, Sweden, Luxembourg and Spain. Not until May 1930 did England and Germany meet in a full international and another three years passed before the first meeting with Italy. In the 1930s, the opposition did come from further afield but only for friendlies. The FA gave the first two World Cup competitions a very wide berth.

There were some nasty shocks for the footballing establishment when England did come up against opposition from outside the United Kingdom.

Although the unbeaten home record against overseas teams was somehow preserved until 1953, inter-war sides had their share of defeats on their travels. Spain were the first to inflict pain, in May 1929, when England lost 4-3 in Madrid. Austria, where Jimmy Hogan was such an influence, managed to hold England to a goalless draw in Vienna in 1930 and then came very close to winning at Stamford Bridge in December 1932. In the end, the hosts scraped a 4-3 win.

Even in the Home Internationals, England did not enjoy unchallenged supremacy. Perhaps Scotland's finest hour was the 5-1 drubbing the Wembley Wizards handed out to England in 1928, when a tiny forward line of Jackson, Dunn, Gallacher, James and Morton destroyed England on a rain-soaked Wembley pitch. In the 1930s, moreover, England won the title outright just once, while Wales managed three wins.

There were, nevertheless, some heroic performances, in particular the triumphs over Italy in 1934 and Germany in 1938, victories over the two leading fascist nations which were welcomed for political as well as sporting reasons. For the match against reigning World Champions Italy at Highbury in November 1934, the English side contained seven Arsenal players (Moss, Male, Hapgood, Copping, Bowden, Drake and Bastin). It was a brutal encounter from which England emerged 3-2 winners.

• Above
The England team give the Nazi salute, Berlin, 1938.

45

Success against Germany came in Berlin in May 1938, at a time when war seemed increasingly likely. Humiliatingly, but on the advice of the British Embassy, the England team gave the Nazi salute beforehand, but it was the only respect they showed the hosts. In an inspired performance, England ran out 6-3 winners.

Yet seven days later, exactly the same England team lost 2-1 to Switzerland in Zurich which showed the flaws in the national side. In an era of so many talented individuals, it was a puzzle that the national side did not do better. Much was made of the fact that the selection committee was made up of club chairman rather than football professionals. A lack of knowledge and favouritism were just two of the selectors' shortcomings. The players themselves, moreover, may have been talented in an English context, but they were found wanting on the international stage.

Jimmy Hogan's unfortunate managerial experiences in England highlighted some of the technical shortcomings which became even more apparent in the post-war era, but which were already evident in the limited exposure the national team had to continental opposition. Just like the 5-1 victory over Germany in the autumn of 2001, the stunning 6-3 success in Berlin in 1938 was a false dawn. The day of football reckoning might have been delayed by the war, but it was just around the corner.

Pre and inter-war greats

Cliff Bastin

An outside-left who played in 392 League and Cup games for Arsenal, scoring 176 goals, he won 21 England caps (12 goals), five League Championship medals, two FA Cup winners and one runners-up medals. Bastin was a 16 year-old plying his footballing trade with unfashionable Exeter City when Herbert Chapman spotted the youngster who was to prove the last major signing of the great side of the 1930s.

He went into the side on Boxing Day 1929 against Portsmouth, finishing the season with 21 League appearances and seven goals. Arsenal were too far behind in the League to challenge, but the FA Cup provided a winning start to Bastin's Highbury career. He scored four goals in the early rounds and won a winner's medal against Huddersfield in April. Bastin was a regular in the Arsenal side that carried off the Championship five times during the next decade, with the 33 goals he scored in season 1932-33 a record for a winger, as well making him Arsenal's top scorer that season.

Bastin's prowess was recognised by England between 1932 and 1937. And, although the Second World War cut short his career, he was still in Arsenal's line-up when League football resumed in 1946-47, the last link with their domination of the 1930s.

Bill 'Dixie' Dean

The most prolific scorer of his day, his 408 goals in 471 League and Cup games included 60 in 39 League games in 1927-28, a record which helped Everton to the League title. He won two League Championship medals and one FA Cup winner's medal, together with 16 England caps.

Born in Birkenhead in 1907, Dean began his career with Tranmere but was soon transferred to Everton. The 1927-28 season was a success for both club and player: his new club won the Championship by two points from Huddersfield and Dean overtook George Camsell's 59-goal record thanks to a hat-trick in the final match against Arsenal. Dean had also missed three games earlier in the season through injury, so his total might have been even higher. As it was he scored over half of Everton's 102 total, a tremendous feat.

Everton were relegated two years later but stormed the Second Division in 1930-31, Dean topping the divisional goalscorers with 39 goals. The following season he won his second League Championship medal and scored 44 goals, again ending the campaign as top scorer in the division. And the Toffees picked up another piece of silverware in 1933, with a 3-0 win over Manchester City in the FA Cup, Dean scoring Everton's second. He finished his League career with Notts County.

Dean maintained an interest in football all his life, and it was perhaps fitting that he should pass away shortly after watching a Merseyside derby in 1980.

• Above
Dixie Dean leaves the Wembley pitch with his Everton colleagues in 1933 with the FA Cup.

Steve Bloomer

Bloomer was a star name at the turn of the twentieth century who set scoring records for club (394 in 655 games for his two clubs) and country (28 for England in 23 games).

From the day he made his League debut for Derby County, Steve Bloomer was scoring goals. There is one record he set that has been equalled, but never beaten; in 1896 he scored five of England's goals in the 9-1 win in Cardiff. Bloomer won little else in the game; Derby reached the FA Cup Final twice during his first spell at the Baseball Ground and twice they returned home defeated; in 1898 3-1 by Nottingham Forest (Bloomer scored Derby's consolation) and 1899, 4-1 by Sheffield United.

Bloomer remained a permanent fixture in Derby's side until 1906 when he was surprisingly allowed to move on to Middlesbrough. There he amassed 59 goals in rather less than five First Division seasons, but returned to Derby (who'd been relegated the year after his departure) in time to help them win promotion from the Second Division as Champions in 1911-12.

It is said the secret of his success was that he did not require much of a backswing with his shooting, which must have made it difficult for goalkeepers to anticipate a shot. Bloomer invariably shot low and was deadly accurate with either foot. That it took three decades for any other player to overtake his haul is testament to his ability.

• Above
Steve Bloomer of Derby and Middlesbrough fame celebrates one of his 23 caps for England.

Charles Buchan

Inside-forward Buchan made 313 first class appearances for Sunderland either side of the First World War, scoring 224 goals before a very unusual transfer to Arsenal. At Highbury he played another 94 games and scored 56 goals. His honours were a Championship medal, two FA Cup runners-up medals and six England caps.

Buchan played as an amateur for Arsenal in his teens, but left and signed professional with Leyton, an expensive mistake for the Gunners. He was transferred to Sunderland in 1911, aged 18, for a fee of £1,200, guiding the club to the League Championship and the Cup Final in 1913 and going on to captain England. Buchan's career might have ended with Sunderland, for he was settled in the area, but Leslie Knighton decided Buchan was the man to strengthen the Arsenal side, offering some £7,000 to take him to Highbury.

Knighton was replaced by Herbert Chapman whose chairman Henry Norris, no mean negotiator, offered £2,000 plus £100 for every goal Buchan scored in his next season – 19 in the League and two in the Cup. Although he played only three seasons at Highbury (he was 34 when he arrived), they were important, transitional seasons for the club that culminated in them reaching their first major Cup Final in 1926-27 (they lost to Cardiff) and making steady progress in the League.

• Above
Arsenal and England's Charles Buchan (left) shows typical determination in a midfield challenge.

• **Above**
Hughie Gallacher, a true Newcastle goalscoring hero with an outstanding strike rate, leads out his team.

Charlie Buchan made 102 appearances for Arsenal in his three seasons, scoring 49 goals. All six of his caps were won while at Sunderland, and he had nothing other than a runners-up medal to show for his time at Arsenal. Yet he remains one of the most important players that ever walked the marble floors of Highbury. When his playing career was over he went into journalism.

Hughie Gallacher

A dynamic, controversial and tragic centre-forward, Gallacher scored 387 goals in 543 League games. He played 20 times for Scotland and won a League Championship medal with Newcastle in 1927.

After starting out with Queen of the South and Airdrie, he joined Newcastle for £6,500, then a record fee for a Scottish player. Newcastle won the title in only his second season with the club and for five years he'd top the Magpies' scoring charts, including 39 in all competitions in Championship season 1926-27.

Temperamental but with a quicksilver footballing mind, he was transferred to Chelsea for a £10,000 fee in 1930. Yet he retained a place in the Gallowgate's communal heart: Newcastle's record attendance in 1930-31 coincided with his visit. By the time he retired in September 1939, he had enjoyed spells with Derby, Notts County, Grimsby and Gateshead.

Gallacher, who had never wanted to leave Newcastle, returned to Tyneside to work in a factory and report on local football. But his private life was in turmoil. Sadly, he committed suicide in 1957, throwing himself under a train. He was just 54.

Billy Meredith

Meredith was the outstanding talent and personality of his era, playing 670 League games for both Manchester clubs (though he is best recalled for his exploits at Old Trafford) and Wales. A winger known as the 'Football Wizard', he was both uniquely talented and highly controversial.

Born in Chirk, North Wales, in 1874, Meredith played for the local team before moving to Northwich Victoria and finally Manchester City in 1894. He played in the first 12 League derbies

between City and United, but was missing from the unlucky 13th, in December 1906. This was due to a huge bribes scandal involving the final game of the previous season, as a result of which 17 players and manager Tom Maley were suspended.

Four of those players, including Meredith, turned their colours and joined United. The result was immediate: the Reds' form improved enough for them to take the title in 1908 and 1911, as well as a Cup win in 1909. He guested for City during the war

• Above
Billy Meredith (right) remains a Manchester legend despite a brush with scandal.

years of 1914-18, while still officially a United player, and rejoined them permanently in 1921 as player-coach. Meredith's second spell at City saw him boost his total for the club to 394 League and Cup appearances, as opposed to 332 for United. His goalscoring ratio was in the Blues' favour, however, having notched 151 for them as opposed to 35 for the Reds.

His international career with Wales started in the 1895 Home Internationals, and would pick up after the First World War to leave him with 48 full caps.

The Post-war UK Boom

Chapter THREE

3

Britain's football-loving public was largely starved of competitive action between 1939 and 1946. During the early days of the war friendly matches were played, but these attracted little interest. Regional leagues were then set up, but the public response was not always terribly enthusiastic. One reason was probably that supporters never knew what, or whom, to expect, as guest players were a common feature of these wartime sides. This was hardly surprising, as men were constantly being called up, and it is a wonder that it was possible to organise football at all. However, the cessation of hostilities was to herald a tremendous boom time for the game.

The 1939-40 season had been brought to a premature close in the September. Most English sides had played just three games and Blackpool were top of the First (top) Division, having taken a maximum six points from their three fixtures. The Scots had started the season earlier, and Rangers headed Division 'A' having secured four wins and a draw.

When the old system was re-established in season 1946-47, Rangers won the Scottish title, finishing two points clear of Hibs, while Liverpool were English champions, finishing just one point clear of Manchester United and Wolves.

In the immediate post-war years, football grounds were very different from those of today. There were no executive boxes (there would have been few executives to fill them) and only the comparatively wealthy chose to sit in the stands, which would have given today's health and safety people apoplexy. Most people stood.

On Saturday afternoons the streets of every major city were thronged with football supporters, almost all male and mostly still wearing caps and smoking Woodbines, on their way to see their teams do battle. Travel to away games was unthinkable for most. If your team was not playing at home, you either went to see the reserves or you went along to the ground of your nearest rivals, perhaps hoping to see them lose. Failing that, you stayed at home and listened to the wireless, and in the evening perhaps you played cards or took your girl to the pictures.

Apart from going to the cinema and watching football, there was little else going on in the world of entertainment – and football was cheap. You could gain access to many grounds for as little as one shilling and threepence (6p) and a programme might cost you 2d or 3d (about 1p). It is true that the facilities were somewhat basic, and the programme was far from being the glossy matchday magazine of today. It is also true that wages were very low, but football was a lot cheaper in real terms than it is today.

And so working men went to football in their tens of thousands. The leading First Division (top-flight) sides attracted crowds in excess of 40,000, week in and week out. The ending of Saturday morning working helped, too.

The average attendance at Wolves' Molineux ground in 1946-47 was 43,000, while Chelsea attracted an average of 46,363 in season 1948-49 and Sunderland an average of 47,785 in 1949-50. Even a modest side playing in the English Second Division could expect regular gates in excess of 20,000. In 1949-50 Sheffield Wednesday's average gate was 40,692 and when Manchester City played Fulham in a Division Two fixture in January 1947, a remarkable 47,658 turned up to watch. Norwich City, playing in Division Three (South) had an average attendance of 23,624 in 1950-51.

• **Opposite**
Servicemen queue for entrance. Once they were demobbed, football became an even more popular pastime.

• **Above**
A wartime England-Scotland international, with forage caps visible among the tam o'shanters and trilbies.

In 1946-47, total attendance figures for first-class football reached 35 million. In 1947-48 it rose to 40 million, generating an income of £4,000,000 – an average of two shillings (10p) per head. The figures include attendances at FA Cup games, internationals and some of the minor leagues, but in 1948-49 more than 41 million people watched League matches alone. This total has never been surpassed.

Footballers were stars and heroes then, as they are today. They were quite well paid by the standards of the time but, until the abolition of the maximum wage in 1961, their wages were very modest by comparison with the stars of stage and screen. After the war, League footballers were entitled to be paid, in addition to their basic wage, a bonus of two pounds for a win, and one pound for a draw. These bonuses were later doubled: riches indeed! When Jimmy Hill, as leader of the players' union, began his campaign for the removal of the maximum wage, it stood at £20 a week (it had been as little as £12 a week in 1947). Twenty pounds a week was a good deal more than the income of the average wage-earner in the early 1960s, but Mr Hill believed top-class footballers were worth a lot more. He was right of course, and the success of his campaign was to lead, almost at once, to a wages explosion.

• Above
Wartime football at the Den in October 1939, Norwich City Millwall's visitors.

• Below
Stanley Matthews takes a corner while playing for the Royal Air Force. Peacetime saw him in more familiar club colours.

To a large extent, English football after the war was very similar to the game that had been played in the 1930s. Many of the same teams continued to battle it out for League and Cup honours, and there was an undying belief that England produced most of the world's best players – a belief not entirely borne out by the statistics. The dominant team of the 1920s had been Huddersfield Town, but they had been usurped in the 1930s by Arsenal. The Gunners had won the First Division title five times between 1930-31 and 1938-39, and had won it three times on the trot in 1932-33, 1933-34 and 1934-35. After the war, their fortunes faded a little, although they did win the League title in 1947-48 and again in 1952-53 – their last League Championship until they achieved the League and Cup Double in 1970-71.

Having won the title at the end of the first post-war season, Liverpool were not to win it again until 1963-64. Portsmouth won the First Division championship in 1948-49, and again the following season when they beat Wolves to the title on goal average. Pompey were always very well supported, with the ranks of supporters swelled by thousands of sailors, and the late 1940s was a very successful era for the club. Having struggled in the top flight for a

few seasons, Portsmouth were relegated to Division Two at the end of the 1958-59 campaign. They finished bottom, nine points behind Aston Villa who went down with them. Pompey were relegated again two seasons later, but returned to the Second Division at the first attempt.

Two clubs dominated the Scottish Division 'A' after the war: Rangers and Hibernian. Rangers won the Scottish championship four times and Hibs won it thrice, before Celtic topped the table at the end of season 1953-54. In England, two clubs dominated the First Division in the 1950s: Manchester United and Wolverhampton Wanderers. Manchester United won the First Division title in 1951-52, 1955-56 and 1956-57. They also won it at the end of 1964-65. Wolves, led by England captain and centre-half Billy Wright, won the First Division title in 1953-54, 1957-58 and 1958-59. Other teams to win the title during this period included Tottenham Hotspur in 1950-51 and 1960-61 (their Double- winning year) and Chelsea, who topped the First Division table in 1954-55.

FA Cup-winning sides have often experienced a mediocre season in the League. This was not the case for Derby County when they beat Charlton Athletic

• **Above**
King George VI presents the first post-war FA Cup to Derby County captain Jack Nicholas, 1946.

4-1 in the 1946 final – because there had been no League season! However, when Charlton took their revenge on the Twin Towers of Wembley the following year, beating Burnley by a goal to nil, they only managed 19th place in the First Division. Charlton's other claim to fame that year was that they had reached the Final having lost a game in an earlier round. In 1946-47 third-round ties were played over two legs and Charlton had been beaten by Fulham at Craven Cottage.

The most successful FA Cup side of the 1940s through to the early 1960s was Newcastle United. They won the trophy three times – in 1951, 1952 and 1955. Manchester United (1948 and 1963), Tottenham Hotspur (1961 and 1962) and Wolves (1949 and 1960) each won it twice. Manchester United were also finalists two years running, in 1957 and 1958.

The 'romance of the Cup' suggests that lower-division sides make it through to the final on a fairly regular basis, but in practice they seldom do. During this period only three Second Division teams reached Wembley and, perhaps sadly, they all lost. When Charlton beat Burnley in 1947, the Lancashire side finished second to Manchester City in Division Two, and were promoted. Two years later, Wolves beat Leicester City in the Final.

Leicester almost completed a unique double by getting to Wembley and being relegated to the Third Division. They finished their season just one point above Nottingham Forest who, together with Lincoln City, had to face the dreaded drop. The only other Second Division team to reach the final during this period was once-proud Preston. They lost 3-2 to West Ham United in 1964, and just missed out on promotion. Doubtless they were quite proud once more, if somewhat miffed.

Between 1947 and 1964 the Scottish FA Cup was won seven times by Rangers, three times each by Aberdeen and Celtic, and once each by Motherwell, Hearts, Falkirk, Clyde and St. Mirren. Overall, there is no doubt that Rangers were the dominant Scottish club side of the immediate post-war period.

Manchester United were arguably the English team of the 1950s but they were to suffer a disaster

of horrific proportions in February 1958, when a plane bringing them home after a European game in Yugoslavia crashed, in icy conditions, on take-off at Munich airport.

Their manager, Matt (later Sir Matt) Busby, had built a magnificent young team which would undoubtedly have won many more honours, but the side was decimated by the crash. Geoffrey Bent, Roger Byrne, Edward Colman, Duncan Edwards, David Pegg, Mark Jones, Billy Whelan and Tommy Taylor all lost their lives, as did Frank Swift, the former Manchester City and England goalkeeper, who was by now a journalist. Matt Busby himself received injuries so serious that it seemed unlikely that he would recover, but recover he did – and he went on to build another team.

• **Above**
Manchester United's wrecked plane, Munich, 1958.

• **Inset**
Manager Matt Busby in an oxygen tent.

• **Below**
The late, legendary and much-missed Duncan Edwards.

Post-war Greats

Stanley Mathews

Ask any older football supporter who was the greatest of them all, and he or she will probably tell you that it was Stanley Matthews. A number of other great post-war players are dealt with in this section, but pride of place has to go to 'the wizard of the dribble'. Stanley, who was born in Hanley, Stoke on 1 February 1915, was the son of a professional boxer.

Matthews made 236 League appearances for his home-town club between 1931 and the outbreak of war. During the conflict, he played in 29 wartime internationals before returning to the First Division with Stoke in 1946. However, after just 23 more League games, he was transferred to Blackpool for the then very substantial fee of £11,500. This came as a terrible shock for the supporters of Stoke City, but Blackpool fans were naturally delighted. Matthews went on to make 379 League appearances for Blackpool before returning to Stoke City in 1961, helping them to promotion back to Division One.

The game that everyone remembers is the one known as the Matthews Final. In 1953, Blackpool reached the Final of the FA Cup, their opponents being Bolton Wanderers. It was a remarkable game, and at one stage Bolton were 3-1 ahead. It seemed to most people watching that his dream of lifting the coveted trophy was lost and gone, but Stanley – and the rest of the Blackpool side – had other ideas. The Seasiders clawed their way back into the game, and finally won it 4-3. Matthews was, naturally, quite magnificent, crossing the ball to Bill Perry for Blackpool's winner, with just 20 seconds left.

Matthews scored on his England debut, when he was just 19. In all, he won 54 full England caps, the last one being awarded when he was aged 42. He was the Footballer of the Year in 1948 and in 1963 (when he was 48) and he was voted European Footballer of the Year in 1956. He played League football past his 50th birthday and he was knighted in 1965 while still a player.

Stanley
Mortensen

At the same time as Matthews, Blackpool had another Stanley – Stan Mortensen. It's little surprise, then, that the Seasiders finished outside the top nine in the First Division only once in the eight seasons between 1946-47 and 1953-54. Mortensen was born at South Shields on 26 May 1921. He made his League debut for Blackpool in the first post-war season and went on to make 317 League appearances, scoring 197 goals.

Although he sometimes occupied an inside-forward position, Mortensen was a centre-forward in the classic mould. He was very quick, totally determined and quite fearless. Although the 1953 FA Cup final will forever be known as the 'Matthews Final' it was Stan Mortensen who scored a hat-trick in that memorable game. Had fantasy football competitions been invented in the 1940s or 1950s, Matthews would have been the king of 'key contributions' while Mortensen would have rattled up the points for his goalscoring prowess.

Stan scored four times against Portugal, in Lisbon, on his England debut in 1947. Admittedly, Portugal were not then the strongest of sides, and

England won 10-0. Nonetheless, it was a remarkable achievement and one would have expected Mortensen to go on to make more than a total of just 25 full appearances, especially as, in those internationals, he scored at a rate of almost a goal a game.

After a sparkling career at Blackpool, Mortensen was transferred, at the age of 34, to Hull City. After a couple of seasons there, he ended his playing days at Southport.

• Opposite
A young Matthews in the colours of home-town club Stoke City with whom he started and finished his career.

• Above
Stan Mortensen, Blackpool's star striker, would feed on Stanley Matthews' crosses in the 1950s.

Sam Bartram

Widely regarded as the finest goalkeeper never to have played for England, although he did feature in three wartime internationals, Sam Bartram was born in Jarrow on 22 January 1914. He was signed for Charlton Athletic by Jimmy Seed in 1934 and, when told he would be paid £5 a week, he thought he was a millionaire.

Bartram made 182 League appearances for Charlton before the war, and a further 397 after it. He was brave, agile and loyal, and he was a spectacular goalkeeper but, as with all spectacular 'keepers, he was prone to the odd crazy error and the odd bad game. Shortly after the war, Charlton had a friendly against Swedish club AIK Stockholm, and Bartram claimed that his colleagues were relieved that the encounter had finished as a seven-all draw!

On the occasion of his 600th appearance for Charlton, Bartram appeared on the pitch to cut a huge celebratory cake. Well, it was different. He then returned north to manage York City, but he will always be remembered at the Valley – Sam Bartram Close is situated near to the ground.

Wilf Mannion

Like Stanley Matthews, Wilf Mannion was an accomplished dribbler. He had a remarkable body-swerve which, again like Matthews, enabled him to leave his opponents standing. Born on Teeside on 16 May 1918, the strong, fair-haired inside-forward was to become the idol of Middlesbrough fans. He made 62 First Division appearances before the war, scoring 18 goals, and went on to make a total of 341 League appearances, scoring just one goal short of a hundred.

Mannion was a player of outstanding ability, and he won representative honours at all levels. In total, he played for England in 26 full internationals, but he could have won many more caps. Indeed, he could have played many more games for Middlesbrough had he not become involved in a contractual dispute during the early 1950s. As employees, footballers had few rights at the time: basically, they were expected to do what they were told. Wilf Mannion's dispute led him to be banned for a period and he lost his place in the England side – a tragedy, because he had formed a wonderful three-way partnership with Stanley Matthews and Nat Lofthouse.

Middlesbrough had refused to release Mannion from his contract, but finally he went to Bury, where he played just 16 League games.

• **Above**
Tees-side idol Wilf Mannion leads out Middlesbrough in 1951.

• **Inset**
Charlton's long-serving keeper Sam Bartram was one of the era's characters.

• **Opposite**
Much-travelled striker Tommy Lawton would have made millions in today's game.

Tommy Lawton

Born in Bolton on 6 October 1919, Tommy Lawton signed professional forms for Burnley on his 17th birthday. After just 25 League games, in which he scored 16 goals, the centre-forward signed for Everton as a replacement for Dixie Dean. They paid £6,500 for his signature, and Lawton scored 34 goals in his new side's Championship-winning season. He was soon picked for England, and in October 1938 he scored from the spot in a match against Wales. In his third international, he headed the winner against Scotland.

The war came when Lawton was at his peak, and probably robbed him of his finest years, but at the cessation of hostilities he decided to move to Stamford Bridge. He scored 26 goals in 34 games for Chelsea, but he became unhappy at the way the club was being run, and so asked for a transfer. He got it and, in November 1947, moved to lowly Notts County for a record fee of £20,000.

Many were amazed that the 28 year-old goalscorer had agreed to join a Third Division club. Lawton was, however, very happy at Meadow Lane, and he went on to score 103 goals in 166 games, helping County to the Third Division (South) championship at the end of the 1949-50 season. He continued to play for his country while he was with Notts County, and in total he played 23 times for England, scoring 22 goals.

Tommy Lawton was in many ways the ideal centre-forward. He was a natural goal-scorer, having a powerful shot and being a remarkably fine header of the ball. Late in his playing career he moved to Brentford, and then to Arsenal. The Gunners signed him to help bring on their youngsters, but Lawton still made 35 League appearances for them.

Billy Liddell

Although many later journeyed south to play for English clubs, there were comparatively few Scots playing English League football immediately after the war.

Billy Liddell was an exception. He was also somewhat exceptional in other ways, becoming both a lay preacher and a Justice of the Peace. Born in Dunfermline on 22 January 1922, he joined Liverpool in 1939, just before the dark clouds gathered, and went on to make nearly 500 appearances for the club, scoring 216 goals in League encounters.

Billy Liddell was an old-fashioned outside-left. For many years he was the idol of the Kop – so much so that the Reds were, for a time, known locally as Liddelpool. He played a significant part in his side's 1946-47 League Championship win and he remained at Anfield until his retirement in 1960, when he proceeded to qualify as an accountant.

Liddell played 28 internationals for Scotland and, apart from Stanley Matthews, was the only footballer to play twice for a Great Britain representative team.

Tom Finney

Tom Finney was born in Preston on 5 April 1922. He joined his only club, Preston North End, as a 15 year-old amateur, and became an apprentice in the plumbing trade. Ever after to be known as the 'Preston Plumber' he laid aside his tools in 1940 and became a professional footballer. It was a wise career move.

A great two-footed player, Finney made his name as a winger during the war and, after only six League games in the 1946-47 season, he won his first England cap. He went on to play in another 75 internationals, scoring 30 times. This was a record then, and Tom Finney is still regarded by many as England's greatest ever wing-forward.

Preston never quite managed to win any titles during the Finney era, so their star player had to be content with runners-up medals. He did not seem to mind. Preston was, and would always be, his team, and he would not have dreamed of playing for any other club. He made 433 League appearances between 1946-47 and 1959-60, scoring 187 goals. Later in his career, Preston converted him into a centre-forward, and, in the 1957-58 season, he scored 26 times.

• **Above left**
Loyal servant Billy Liddell was Liverpool's biggest name in the pre-Shankly era.

• **Above right**
Preston and England's Tom Finney shows his skill on the ball.

Tom Finney was twice voted Footballer of the Year and, in 1998, he received a somewhat belated knighthood for his services to football. Later, in February 2000, a statue modelled on the photograph of an incident at Stamford Bridge in 1956 in which Finney controlled a pass from team-mate Tommy Docherty in appallingly wet conditions, was unveiled at the National Football Museum at Preston's Deepdale ground. The sculpture is called 'The Splash'. Tom Finney certainly made a splash at Preston North End.

Billy Wright

Billy Wright was another one-club man. Although he was from the Midlands, he had supported Arsenal as a boy. However, when Wolverhampton Wanderers advertised for trialists at Molineux, he decided to apply. Born at Ironbridge on 6 February 1924, he was taken up by Wolves and played his first 'B' team game at the early age of 14. Even so, his manager, Major Frank Buckley, told him that, in his opinion, Billy was not going to make it as a professional footballer. He was wrong. Very wrong.

Billy Wright turned professional in 1941. He played more than 100 wartime games for Wolves, as both a forward and a defender, and he also made a few guest appearances for Leicester City. He played as a wing-half for Wolves in the first post-war season, and was appointed captain when Stan Cullis retired in 1947. He went on to make 490 League appearances, as either a wing-half or a centre-half, before his retirement in 1959, when he held the League Championship trophy aloft for the third time in his career.

In-between times, Wright made 105 appearances for England (90 of them as captain) – a record which was to stand until Bobby Charlton played his one hundred and sixth match in 1970. Wright's first full international was a 1-1 draw against Scotland at Wembley, in 1947; his last an 8-1 defeat of the United States in Los Angeles in 1959. At one stage he had a run of 46 consecutive England games.

Billy Wright was an inspirational captain of both club and country. His conversion to the centre-half position was all the more remarkable because he stood only 5 feet 8 inches, but he made up for his lack of stature by keeping the ball on the ground as much as possible. He was awarded the OBE at the end of his playing career and his funeral, in 1994, brought the centre of Wolverhampton to a standstill.

• **Above**
Billy Wright, in the old gold of Wolves, evades a last-ditch tackle.

Jackie Milburn

Although he played only 13 times for England, his first international call-up being in 1948, Jackie Milburn was a Tyneside hero. Born at Ashington on 11 May 1924, he signed as a professional for Newcastle United in August 1943. He played either at outside-right, or in the middle, and he combined a shot like a rocket with tremendous acceleration.

'Wor Jackie' was to score 177 League goals in 353 appearances, but it was in the FA Cup that he really made a name for himself. Newcastle won the trophy three times while he was in the side. Milburn scored both goals in the final against Blackpool in 1951 and, four years later against Manchester City, he headed a fine goal in a 3-1 Wembley victory. Altogether, he scored on 22 occasions in Cup ties. Jackie Milburn's other claim to fame is that he was Bobby and Jack Charlton's uncle.

• **Above**
Jackie Milburn, pictured at Wembley in 1955, played three times in Cup Finals in Newcastle's colours.

Jimmy Dickinson

'Gentleman Jim' Dickinson was born in Alton, Hampshire, on 24 April 1925. After three years in the Royal Navy, he made his League debut for Portsmouth in the first post-war season. It was to be the first of 764 League games for Pompey.

Together with fellow half-backs Jack Froggatt and Jimmy Scoular, Dickinson guided Pompey to two successive League championships. At the time, these three formed probably the best half-back line in the country. Dickinson was elegant and sure-footed and he worked extremely hard. He was known as a gentleman both on and off the field. Referees were less inclined than they are today to reach for their pencils at the first sign of an illegal challenge, but most defenders received a few bookings during their careers. Not so, Dickinson: his name was never taken during his League or international career and he was, of course, never sent off.

Jimmy Dickinson made 48 appearances in an England shirt, playing at left-half. He would probably have added to this total had Portsmouth not decided to turn him into a centre-half, a move which cost him his place in the international team. His last appearance for Pompey was in 1965, in a 1-1 draw with Northampton which prevented Portsmouth from being relegated to the Third Division.

Gentleman Jim later managed Portsmouth for a short while. Unfortunately, the strains of managing a club in decline did nothing for his health, and he died at the early age of 57.

Nat Lofthouse

Nat Lofthouse was possibly the most feared centre-forward of his time. Born in Bolton on 27 August 1925, he more or less followed Tommy Lawton into his local school side. Unlike Lawton, Lofthouse joined his local professional club and stayed there until injury finally ended his career in 1960. In his 14 seasons with Bolton Wanderers, he made 503 League and Cup appearances, and scored 285 goals – a club record.

• **Above**
Jimmy Dickinson, a Portsmouth legend whose unblemished disciplinary record is an example to others.

• **Above**
Nat Lofthouse shows off the FA Cup won in 1958 by his brace of goals.

• **Opposite**
Johnny Haynes, 'The Maestro', displays his ball skills at Fulham's Craven Cottage ground.

Lofthouse is Bolton's favourite son. He played in the 1953 FA Cup final against Blackpool and, although he finished on the losing side in that dramatic encounter, he was voted Footballer of the Year. Five years later, in 1958, Bolton again reached Wembley. This time they won the trophy, beating local rivals Manchester United 2-0 . Lofthouse scored both goals, and is remembered for shoulder-charging the United keeper into the net. You could do that sort of thing in those days.

Known as the 'Lion of Vienna' after he scored a dramatic goal against Austria, Nat Lofthouse played for England on 33 occasions, scoring 30 goals. Having lost his place in the England side, he made a come-back at the age of 35, shortly before his retirement, when he played against the USSR and Wales.

Johnny Haynes

Johnny Haynes was born in Edmonton, north London on 17 October 1934. He was to become one of the outstanding inside-forwards of the era. Arsenal and Spurs wanted to sign him, but Haynes joined Fulham, making his first-team debut on Boxing Day 1952. He went on to play a total of 657 matches in all competitions, scoring 157 goals, before his retirement from English football in 1970. His goal tally was all the more remarkable because he was, in theory at least, a provider rather than a scorer, and yet his total was not bettered by any Fulham player until Gordon Davies exceeded it in 1989.

Haynes had magnificent distribution and control, and he dictated play from midfield for almost twenty years. For much of this time the Cottagers were in the Second Division, and it was a wonder to many that he did not move on. He stayed at Fulham, however, and, following the abolition of the maximum wage, he became Britain's first £100 a week footballer. Haynes did sometimes become frustrated, especially when team-mates failed to run into spaces to collect his superb passes or through-balls, but he was forced to accept that others had far less talent than himself.

Johnny Haynes played for England on 56 occasions, 22 of them as captain. His greatest game was against Russia in 1958, when his hat-trick helped England to a 5-0 victory. He also featured in England's 9-3 beating of Scotland at Wembley in 1961, where his creative midfield play was inspirational. His England career ended with the 1962 World Cup Finals – a car crash, which kept him out of the game for some time, costing him his place thereafter. After leaving Fulham, he played football in South Africa. Johnny Haynes now lives in Edinburgh, where he plays golf and supports Heart of Midlothian.

There were of course many more great players in those post-war years. Three wing-halves who came to prominence during this period were Joe Mercer, Danny Blanchflower and Ron Flowers. Mercer actually came to prominence before the war, having played in the England side before hostilities commenced. He spent much of the 1930s with Everton, before joining Arsenal in December 1946. A serious knee injury limited his international appearances and threatened his career but he somehow kept going until a broken leg finally forced him into retirement in 1954. He later became a great manager, most notably at Manchester City.

Danny Blanchflower was signed by Barnsley from Glentoran in April 1949, for a £6,500 fee. He later moved to Aston Villa, but it was with Tottenham Hotspur that he attained lasting fame and glory. He was Spurs' skipper in 1960-61, when they won the Double, and he played 56 times for Northern Ireland. When he retired from football, he took up journalism. He also advertised Shredded Wheat on television.

Ron Flowers featured in the great Wolves side of the 1950s. Strong and well-built, he was often likened to the Wolves' other accomplished wing-half, Billy Wright. Flowers appeared 49 times in an England shirt, and as well as contributing to Wolves' glory days, he did much to prop them up when they became less successful.

Roger Byrne started out as an outside-left, before converting to the left-back position. He spent his entire professional career with Manchester United, a career tragically cut short in the Munich disaster. By February 1958 he had played 33 times for England. Had he survived, he would doubtless have won many more caps.

Two goalscorers who made their mark after the war, were Len Shackleton and Roy Bentley. Shackleton, known as the 'clown prince of soccer' for his desire always to entertain the crowd, played for England on just five occasions. However, he scored 26 goals in 57 League games for Newcastle, and 98 in 320 for Sunderland. Roy Bentley was a roving centre-forward possessing all the attributes needed by a goalscorer. His England appearances were limited to 12, but he played in 512 League games, 324 of which were for Chelsea. He also played for Fulham and Queens Park Rangers, and in all he netted 173 League goals.

Three outstanding goalkeepers are worthy of mention. Bert Williams shone in wartime football and was signed by Wolves from Walsall in 1945. Known as 'The Cat', he succeeded Frank Swift in the England jersey. Williams played for his country on 24 occasions, while Jack Kelsey of Arsenal played for his 41 times. Welshman Kelsey was a former blacksmith.

• **Above**
Len Shackleton, unusually a hero for both Newcastle and Sunderland.

• **Right**
Bert Williams, known as 'The Cat', gets down on all fours to save.

• **Opposite**
John Charles rises to clear the danger.

He was very agile on the goal line and the highlight of his career must have been when Wales reached the quarter-finals of the World Cup in 1958.

Meanwhile, there was Bert Trautmann. He was not eligible to play for any of the home countries, having been a German prisoner of war. Any prejudice against him was soon overcome, however, and he proved to be a marvellous 'keeper for Manchester City, going on to make well over 500 appearances for them. He will always be remembered for breaking his neck in the 1956 FA Cup final against Birmingham, and for refusing to leave the field. As far as he was concerned, worse things had happened during the war.

Two pairs of brothers loomed large not too long after the war, and both pairs came from Swansea. The Allchurch brothers – Ivor and Len – both began, and ended, their careers with Swansea Town. In-between times, Ivor played for Newcastle and Cardiff, while Len played for Sheffield United and Stockport County. Ivor was a perceptive, ball-playing inside-forward who scored more than 250 League goals between 1949 and 1967, while Len mainly played at outside-right. Len was less prolific on the goal-scoring front, but he was nonetheless an outstanding player. He played 11 times for Wales, while Ivor notched up 68 appearances.

John and Mel Charles were born in Swansea, but John never played for his home-town side. Instead, the centre-forward joined Leeds United, and in season 1953-54 he scored a remarkable 42 League goals for the Second Division team. John Charles was an early footballing export and in 1957 he joined Juventus for a record £65,000 fee. He later played for Roma and Cardiff City.

Mel was always in the shadow of his big brother, but he joined Swansea and scored 69 goals in 233 League appearances between 1952 and 1959. He was then signed by Arsenal, where he never really settled, even though he continued to score freely, and later played for Cardiff City and Port Vale. John played 38 times for Wales, while Mel won 31 caps.

Another pair of very famous footballing brothers came along a little later – the Charltons. Jackie was a tall centre-half, and made 628 League appearances for Leeds United between 1952 and 1973. He did not force his way into the England team until 1964, but he then earned 35 caps. He became a manager when he stopped playing, and eventually took charge of the Republic of Ireland team.

• **Above**
*World Cup-winning
brothers Bobby
and Jack Charlton
in the colours of
their country.*

Born at Ashington on 11 October 1937, Bobby Charlton was with Manchester United from 1954 until 1974. Famous for his amazing shooting ability, he came to prominence in the Manchester United team fashioned after Munich. He won countless honours, including 106 England caps – and, together with brother Jackie, the greatest prize of all: a World Cup winner's medal.

Other stars of the later post-war era include inside-forwards Denis Law and Jimmy Greaves. Law was capped by Scotland 55 times. He played for Huddersfield, Manchester City and Manchester United, where he scored 171 goals in 305 League matches between 1962 and 1973. In-between times, he also went to Italy, for a single season with Torino.

Greaves is noted as being the greatest goalscorer of modern times – he scored 124 in 157 League appearances for Chelsea, and a further 220 in 321 League games for Tottenham. He played 57 times for England, but is probably best remembered (other than by Chelsea and Spurs fans) for being left out of the 1966 World Cup final. This is a pity, because he was absolutely brilliant.

Finally, a brief mention of three more players who made significant contributions to British football prior to and, in two cases, during, the events of 1966. Firstly, England skipper Bobby Moore (christened Robert Frederick Chelsea Moore –

someone got it just a little bit wrong!) who was one of the finest central defenders ever to grace a football field. Moore made more than 650 League appearances, mainly for West Ham United, and played for England on 108 occasions. He even won an FA Cup medal, albeit a loser's one, when playing for Fulham in the twilight of his career in 1975.

Gordon Banks, of Chesterfield, Leicester City and Stoke, was widely acknowledged as one of the world's finest goalkeepers, and he was of course another hero of the 1966 World Cup. His technique was superb and he had great powers of concentration. Sadly, his career was cut short by a motoring accident in 1972.

Last but not least must be mentioned George Best, the Belfast boy who blossomed into arguably the greatest footballing talent the British Isles ever produced. Plucked from obscurity at 15 by Manchester United boss Matt Busby, who saw in him the spirit of his tragic Babes, the young wing wizard was blooded in the League two years later in September 1963 and went on to play 26 times that season, soon winning an international debut for Northern Ireland. A legend was born.

Championship honours followed in the 1964-65 season, by which time Best was front-page news. Young, glamorous and successful, he set trends in fashion and hairstyles off the pitch and bewildered

opponents on it with his ball control, searing pace and the strength of a natural athlete.

George ended the 1967-68 European Cup season with 32 goals, the Footballer of the Year trophy and the prestigious European Player of the Year award. But the disruptive side of genius was already beginning to surface, and when Busby stepped down in 1969 the one influential figure in Best's life went with him.

After years of squabbling over drinking bouts, non-appearances and domestic upheavals, Best finally walked out of Old Trafford for good in 1973 having scored 178 goals in 466 games. His comparative absence from the international scene – just 37 caps and no World Cup Finals – remains a travesty. A self-declared alcoholic, Best had forgettable comeback spells with a host of clubs but

will always be remembered in his prime as one of the world's great footballing stars. Having successfully survived a 2002 liver transplant, he remains in demand as a TV football pundit.

The immediate post-war era was a great one for British football. The game had some marvellous players and there was a belief among the English public that their football was the best in the world. There were, however, warning signs. Before the war, the South Americans had started to get in on the act, and after it European football began to improve rapidly.

England, who had never taken the World Cup very seriously, were beaten 1-0 by the USA in 1950, but nobody (except a few Americans) took much notice. However, in 1953, Hungary came to Wembley and gave the English side a lesson in football. They

• Above
George Best in offensive action for Manchester United against Chelsea.

73

won 6-3, the first time England had been beaten at Wembley. Worse was to follow when, a year later, Hungary ran out 7-1 winners in Budapest and, although England still seldom lost on home territory, there were further Wembley defeats in 1959 (Sweden) and 1965 (Austria).

England did have a very good side by the time of the 1966 World Cup, and they did magnificently to win the trophy, even if a Russian linesman was called upon to make a significant contribution. But it would all be a lot harder from then on.

England's Finest Hour

Chapter
FOUR
4

Even if they are too young to remember it personally, every supporter of England's national team has to admit their finest hour remains the World Cup victory over West Germany at Wembley in 1966. It not only set the seal on very nearly a century of international competition, but has presented a punishing benchmark for successive teams and managers to live up to.

England's first seven international fixtures were against Scotland. As briefly recounted in our first chapter, the series began on 30 November 1872 when 4,000 expectant Scotsmen saw the countries play out a goalless draw at Hamilton Crescent, Glasgow. Undeterred by this less than promising start, the gentlemen of England invited the Scots to compete again, this time at the Kennington Oval in March 1873. About 3,000 expectant Englishmen viewed this one, and were no doubt thrilled by a 4-2 victory for the home team.

After five more international fixtures against Scotland, the English invited Wales to the Oval in January 1879, when the visitors were beaten 2-1. Ireland were beaten 13-0 in Belfast in 1882, but the home international series, as such, did not get under way until the 1883-84 season. It was to last for a hundred years and for much of that time the matches played assumed paramount importance for the England team. This is hardly surprising as, in the early days at least, hardly anyone outside these islands was playing the game at international level.

England's first match against 'foreign' opposition did not come until 1908, when Austria were beaten 6-1 in Vienna on 6 June. The fixture was repeated two days later, and this time England won 11-1, with four goals from Viv Woodward and three from Tom Bradshaw. Two days after that, England were in Budapest, beating Hungary 7-0, and George Hilsdon scored four of them.

Professionalism had come about gradually during the latter part of the nineteenth century, and with it the development of the game we know today. In the early part of the twentieth century, the England side reigned supreme on the international front and, even after the horrors of the Great War, there were few teams to touch them.

There were, however, fewer big wins after World War I. Still, in March 1923 England beat Belgium 6-1 at Highbury, and in May 1927 they beat them again, this time 9-1. Dixie Dean scored a hat-trick in that match and, ten days later, he scored another in a 5-2 victory in Luxembourg. He only scored two when England beat France 6-0 in Paris on 25 May.

In December 1931 England beat Spain 7-1 at Highbury. Dean managed only a single goal but John Smith, Joe Johnson and Sam Crooks scored two apiece. By 1934 cracks were beginning to show. Even with the likes of Eddie Hapgood and Cliff Bastin in the team, England were beaten 2-1 in both Hungary and Czechoslovakia. Their home record was still very good but more war clouds heralded a dark time ahead for English international football.

England played a total of 36 unofficial wartime international games between 1939 and 1946: 16 of these were against Scotland, and 15 against Wales. Northern Ireland, Belgium, Switzerland and France (twice) also featured. The first match was against Wales at Ninian Park in November 1939; it attracted a crowd numbering 28,000 and finished 1-1. The last was a Victory International against France, played in Paris during May 1946. A total of 58,481 Frenchmen turned out for this one. Perhaps they were grateful for liberation but their team showed no gratitude whatsoever by beating England 2-1.

Although the English have traditionally regarded the Scots as their strongest home-country opponents, it was Wales that proved to be more formidable opposition during the war years. The Principality beat England four times during this period, while Scotland only managed three victories against the Auld Enemy. Nonetheless, the English sides did well enough during their 36 encounters, winning 22, drawing 6 and losing 8. They also scored 98 goals and conceded just 49. A total of 78 players were called into action, many of them having already seen action of a different kind.

• Opposite
Gordon Banks punches clear during an Argentine attack in the 1966 World Cup quarter-final.

• Above
A mass of patriotic fervour as England and Scotland go head to head in 1948.

• **Above**
The urbane Walter Winterbottom, England's first manager who, bizarrely, had his team selected for him by committee.

Team selection was a problem. Players thought to be available suddenly became unavailable, and last-minute substitutions sometimes had to be made. This even resulted oddities such as a Scotsman, Tommy Pearson of Newcastle, playing for England against his own country. All the same, the quality of football was high and attendances were remarkable: in April 1945, 133,000 people turned up at Hampden Park to see Scotland beaten 6-1 by England.

England's biggest victory during the period was an 8-0 drubbing of Scotland at Maine Road, in October 1943. The England team, thought to be one of the finest for many years, comprised: Frank Swift, Laurie Scott, George Hardwick, Cliff Britton, Stan Cullis, Joe Mercer, Stanley Matthews, Raich Carter, Tommy Lawton, Jimmy Hagan and Dennis Compton. In that game, Lawton scored four times. England had beaten Wales 8-3 during the previous month, and were in the middle of a run of 15 games in which they were unbeaten.

Officially, wartime football came to an end at the start of the 1946-47 League season. Many players had, sadly, lost their best years to the conflict but many were also to make their names in internationals played during the late 1940s.

Walter Winterbottom became the England manager in 1946. He came in for a fair amount of criticism during his long reign, but his record of 79 victories, 32 draws and 28 defeats in 139 international matches, was far from a bad one. His critics accused him of a lack of understanding of the professional game, believing that he had gained little or no experience as a player. He had in fact played for Manchester United, where he made just 27 appearances as a half-back (midfielder) before spinal problems forced him into early retirement in 1938.

Winterbottom was born in Oldham, and he was only 33 years old when he took over the England team. He had already been a schoolmaster and a lecturer at the Carnegie Physical Education College

and, during the war, he had served with the Royal Air Force as a wing commander. So it was felt that Wing Commander Winterbottom was an all-round 'good egg', just the sort of chap to lead the English on battlefields new.

His upper lip was as stiff as they came, and although he had not managed at club level, he knew all about football. So he was appointed as the Football Association's Director of Coaching, as well as manager of the country's amateur and professional sides. It would be fair to say that not everyone agreed this essentially middle-class gentleman was the right man to head up England's footballing challenge to the world, but it would also be fair to say that, given all the circumstances, his critics were probably wrong.

He was a very good coach, and as well as establishing a national coaching scheme, he also set up England's youth and Under-23 teams. He was probably hampered by the fact that, although he was the England manager, he was not allowed to select the team. He certainly exerted his influence in this respect, especially towards the end of his tenure, but teams were still chosen by a committee.

Winterbottom experienced ups and downs, successes and failures, and he was in charge for a remarkable 16 years, finally giving up his post in 1962. He knelt before the Queen in 1978, and Sir Walter Winterbottom died, aged 89, in February 2002.

Winterbottom had inherited some excellent players after the war. His, and England's, first

• Above

Winterbottom talks tactics with members of the England team training at Highbury for a match against Sweden in 1959.

postwar 'official' international was a Home Championship match in Northern Ireland, played on 28 September 1946. It resulted in a 7-2 victory for the visitors, with Wilf Mannion scoring a hat-trick.

After a 1-0 victory over the Republic of Ireland in a friendly two days later, England's next game was against Wales in October. It resulted in a 3-0 win at Maine Road, Wilf Mannion scoring two more goals, Tommy Lawton getting the other. The England team was the same for all three games, and there was only one change – Herbert Johnston taking over the Number 6 shirt from Cockburn – when they beat Holland at Leeds Road, Huddersfield, by eight goals to two, in November. Six months on, eight members of the same side were present when England travelled to Lisbon to engage Portugal, and beat them 10-0. Cockburn, Finney and Carter were absent, replaced by Eddie Lowe, together with the two Stanleys – Matthews and Mortensen.

The internationals played during the late 1940s were all either against the home countries, or friendlies against European opposition. One other notable result came in a game against Italy in Turin, during May 1948. The team adopted a surprisingly positive attitude in this difficult game, with an emphasis on attack. It worked and, with Tom Finney playing on the left wing and Matthews on the right, England ran out 4-0 winners. Their scorers were Finney (2), Lawton and Mortensen.

When Uruguay had won the World Cup in 1930, and Italy had won it in 1934 and again in 1938, England had not bothered to enter the competition. This was almost certainly a mistake so, when the year 1950 was selected for the re-start of the competition, England decided to put in an appearance. In retrospect, this was probably a mistake too, as the evidence suggests that the English football authorities were still not taking the competition very seriously.

The 1950 World Cup finals were held in Brazil, and England started brightly enough by beating Chile 2-0 (Mortensen and Mannion). The Brazilians were well on the way to emerging as a great team, and would later reach the Final, but England supporters expected their side to do equally well. They were, however, inexplicably beaten 1-0 by the USA and then beaten, also 1-0, by Spain. Even with the likes of Billy Wright, Tom Finney and Stan

Mortensen in the side, it was clear that England was no longer the supreme footballing nation, so it was back to the Home International Championship and a plethora of friendlies.

One of those came in November 1953, when Ferenc Puskas and his Mighty Magyars overcame England at Wembley. The 6-3 scoreline stunned everyone and perhaps no-one more than England right-back Alf Ramsey. Could it be that at this moment Ramsey decided that radical changes in tactics would one day be needed? At all events, the following year saw no improvement in England's fortunes. Hungary won the return fixture 7-1, and then England made another early exit from the World Cup. They drew 4-4 with Belgium, beat the host nation, Switzerland, 2-0 in Berne, and then went down 4-2 to Uruguay at the quarter-final stage.

The European Nations Cup did not get underway until 1960 (and even then, England decided not to enter) and so it was only in the World Cup that the side could seriously test its strength against other nations. It usually did well in the qualifying matches, and this was again the case prior to the 1958 finals. Having beaten Denmark twice and the Republic of Ireland once, Walter Winterbottom's boys journeyed to Sweden full of hope, and began their campaign in the finals with a 2-2 draw against the USSR. This was followed by a creditable goalless draw with Brazil, and a rather less creditable 2-2 draw with Austria.

By now, the team had seen many changes, the line-up for the game against Brazil being: Colin McDonald, Don Howe, Tommy Banks, Eddie Clamp, Billy Wright, Bill Slater, Bryan Douglas, Bobby Robson, Derek Kevan, Johnny Haynes and Alan

• **Above**
The England team arrives back at London's Heathrow Airport from Rio after failure in the 1950 World Cup.

A'Court. Three draws were not enough to secure a place in the quarter-finals, so a play-off with the USSR was required. Unfortunately, England this time went down by a goal to nil.

By the end of the 1950s everyone knew that England were no longer the kings of the game, and had not in fact reigned for some considerable time – even though they did defeat a depleted Scotland side 9-3 in April 1961, with a hat-trick from Jimmy Greaves and a couple each from Bobby Smith and Johnny Haynes. Walter Winterbottom was to have one last go at real glory in 1962, when his team travelled to Chile.

The bankrupt South American country was a surprise choice as a venue for the finals of the World Cup, but Chile actually organised the tournament very well, even constructing two magnificent new stadiums. England, however, failed fairly miserably. They enjoyed only one success in their group games, when they beat Argentina 3-1 with goals from Ron Flowers, Bobby Charlton and Jimmy Greaves, but they lost to Hungary (2-1) and Brazil (3-1). They did, however, get a 0-0 draw with Bulgaria, and managed to scrape into the quarter-finals, where they lost 3-1 to Brazil.

It was time for Walter to quit his post, and in January 1963 Alf Ramsey became the England manager. Ramsey, born in Dagenham on 22 January 1920, had played League football for Southampton and Tottenham. As an intelligent and polished defender, he had played for his country on 32 occasions. As manager of Ipswich Town, he had

guided the Suffolk club from Division Three (South) to the championship of Division One – then the top division – in just five years, a quite remarkable achievement.

Ramsey's achievements at Ipswich were all the more remarkable because he had spent little on strengthening his squad. He had relied instead on motivation and on the building of team spirit. His tactics were innovative and he was not terribly interested in 'star' players. He relied on teamwork and he expected commitment and complete loyalty from his players. In return, he would defend the interests of his players, come what may.

Alf Ramsey was the first full-time England manager and, crucially, was given total control over team selection. He would not have had it any other way. He was not terribly interested in what the press had to say about him, and this was probably just as well because, up until 1966, he bore his fair share of criticism. Ramsey was taciturn, speaking to reporters only when there was no avoiding them. He was regarded as a somewhat colourless character and his outburst after England's 1966 World Cup quarter-final match against Argentina, when he referred to

• Opposite
England prepare to battle Brazil in the 1962 World Cup in Chile.

• Above
The impassive Alf Ramsey, a taciturn man but a tactically aware manager.

• Below
Ramsey addresses Barry Bridges, Jack Charlton and Nobby Stiles in 1965. Note the tracksuit as opposed to Winterbottom's overcoat.

• Above
Gordon Banks foils Mexico's Navarro en route to England's 2-0 first-round win, 1966.

the opposition as having played "like animals", seemed out of character. He was, however, always extremely passionate about the game and, in reality, criticism hurt him deeply.

At Ipswich, Ramsey had largely abandoned the use of wingers in favour of forwards who were versatile, had a high work-rate, and were prepared to scrap. He carried over this philosophy into the England side, and was duly criticised for producing teams designed to bore the most dedicated supporter to tears. But, of course, it worked.

Ramsey's first game in charge of England was a European Nations Cup qualifying match in Paris. It resulted in a 5-2 defeat at the hands of France, and, as the teams had drawn 1-1 in Sheffield before Ramsey took over, it meant that England were out of the competition at the first attempt. Ramsey's team comprised: Ron Springett, Jimmy Armfield, Ron

Henry, Bobby Moore, Brian Labone, Ron Flowers, John Connelly, Bobby Tambling, Bobby Smith, Jimmy Greaves and Bobby Charlton. Ramsey's second game also resulted in defeat, this time by Scotland (2-1) at Wembley, but during the remainder of 1963 his side went seven games without losing.

Over the next two years, Ramsey began building a team for an assault on the Jules Rimet Trophy in 1966. The World Cup finals were to be played in England, so the host nation qualified automatically. This was of great assistance to the manager: he could experiment in friendlies and home internationals, where the results were of comparatively minor significance. During 1964, players such as Gordon Banks, Ray Wilson, Bobby Moore, Roger Hunt and Bobby Charlton all made regular international appearances. In 1965, they were joined by Jack Charlton, Alan Ball and Nobby Stiles.

All of these were later to play in the World Cup final, with only one player, Geoff Hurst, yet to come to prominence during this two-year period.

England were to play a total of 17 matches during 1966, although only the most optimistic supporter would have expected so many. The first game was a friendly against Poland, played at Goodison Park in January. The team – Banks, Cohen, Wilson, Stiles, Jack Charlton, Moore, Ball, Hunt, Baker, Eastham and Harris – drew 1-1, with Bobby Moore scoring England's goal. Gordon Harris was a winger (presumably no-one told Alf!) from Burnley, and this was to be his only England appearance.

There were just three changes for the next match, a friendly against West Germany which England won 1-0 at Wembley. Keith Newton, Geoff Hurst and Bobby Charlton were in, while Ray Wilson, George Eastham and Gordon Harris were omitted. England's scorer was Nobby Stiles. The England side contained nine of the players who were to feature against West Germany in the World Cup final later in the year. By contrast, only five of the West German players – goalkeeper Hans Tilkowski, plus Willi Schulz, Wolfgang Weber, Franz Beckenbauer and Siegfried Held – were to play in that memorable match.

Having beaten Scotland 4-3 at Hampden Park, and also Yugoslavia (2-0) at Wembley, England went on a short Scandinavian tour before the World Cup finals began. The first game produced another clean sheet for goalkeeper Gordon Banks, as the tourists

overcame Finland 3-0, and this was followed by a 6-1 victory over Norway, in which Jimmy Greaves netted four times, before Denmark were beaten 2-0. This was all very encouraging, and there was further encouragement in the shape of a 1-0 victory over Poland in Chorzow on 5 July. Just six days later, the real work began.

England were drawn in Group One for the World Cup finals, along with France, Mexico and Uruguay. A good start was important, and Alf Ramsey selected the following side for the opening game against

• **Above**
Bobby Moore in action against the 'animals' of Argentina.

• **Below**
Portugal's Eusebio leaves the field in tears after his country's 2-1 semi-final defeat, 1966.

Uruguay, at Wembley, on 4 July:

Gordon Banks, the Leicester City 'keeper who had by now made the England Number 1 shirt his own.

George Cohen, the Fulham right-back who, because of his tremendous speed, was a natural choice for Ramsey's 'wingless wonders'.

Ray Wilson, Everton's hard-tackling, constructive and reliable left back.

Nobby Stiles, the Manchester United wing-half with the toothy grin and indomitable spirit: the hard man of the side.

Jackie Charlton, the Leeds United centre-half, known to many as the 'giraffe'.

Bobby Moore, the cultured central defender from West Ham, who was the team captain.

Alan Ball, the Blackpool midfield player with tremendous energy.

Roger Hunt, the Liverpool inside-forward with excellent shooting skills.

John Connelly, an outside-right from Manchester United.

Jimmy Greaves, the inside-forward from Tottenham Hotspur, who was the most prolific goalscorer of his time.

Bobby Charlton of Manchester United, younger brother of Jackie and another forward with exceptional shooting power.

Uruguay were not the footballing force that they had been a decade or more earlier, but they managed to prevent England from scoring on this occasion. More than 87,000 people witnessed a 0-0 draw and, although England were still very much in the World Cup, this was not the most auspicious of beginnings.

Ramsey made two changes for the game against Mexico, Ball and Connelly making way for Terry Paine, the speedy, two-footed Southampton winger, and West Ham's Martin Peters, a midfielder with outstanding talent and superb passing skills. Undeterred by England's failure to score against Uruguay, 92,570 souls turned up at Wembley. They were lucky. Goals from Bobby Charlton and Roger Hunt secured a 2-0 victory, leaving only France to be drawn with or beaten if England were to be sure of a place in the quarter-finals.

Wembley was almost full for the game against the French. Only one team change was made this time, Liverpool's Ian Callaghan coming in for Terry Paine. It seemed that Ramsey was having trouble accepting any kind of traditional winger in his side,

and Callaghan was not to feature in the remaining three games. Roger Hunt was fast becoming the man of the tournament as far as England were concerned. The direct and resourceful '90-minute man' who had scored against Mexico now added another two against France. Banks once more kept a clean sheet – and England were in the quarter-finals.

Portugal, North Korea, the USSR, Hungary, West Germany, Uruguay and Argentina were the other quarter-finalists. There is almost always a surprise team in any tournament and this time it was North Korea, who had effectively knocked out mighty Italy in one of the most remarkable victories in World Cup history. Brazil had started out as favourites but had failed to reach the last eight, star forward Pele complaining bitterly about the lack of protection awarded him by referees during the tournament.

England's quarter-final opponents were Argentina. Alan Ball came back into the side to replace Ian Callaghan, and there was one other change – Geoff Hurst, a third West Ham player, came in for Jimmy Greaves. Greaves was injured but, in spite of his remarkable goalscoring ability, he was just not Ramsey's kind of player and did not fit into the manager's philosophy. Hurst, on the other hand,

was unselfish as well as being an accomplished target-man. It was, some said, a triumph of efficiency over genius.

The game against Argentina was not a pretty one to watch. At the end of a bruising 90 minutes, many of the 90,584 people watching probably agreed with the sentiments expressed by the normally placid England manager. Antonio Rattin had got his marching orders, Geoff Hurst had got onto the scoresheet and England had won by that single goal but Ramsey was furious and refused to let his players exchange shirts with their opponents after the match.

But England were in the semi-finals.

For the game against Portugal, Ramsey made no changes to his team, even though Greaves was rumoured to be fully fit. Hurst had scored the only goal against Argentina and was fitting so well into the formation that the manager saw no need to bring Greaves back.

The Portuguese side was undoubtedly one of the best in the World Cup Finals, even if the defence was at times a little suspect. Eusebio had netted four times in the 5-3 quarter-final defeat of North Korea, and he was to finish as the top scorer with nine

• **Above**
3-2! Roger Hunt acclaims Geoff Hurst's first extra-time strike.

strikes in all. His last goal came in the semi-final, as his side was to exit the competition with England's 2-1 victory. Portugal – whose team comprised José Pereira, Festa, Batista, Carlos, Hilario, Jaime Graca, Coluna, Jose Augusto, Eusebio, Torres and Simoes – fought hard in what was to be a tremendous game of football, but they could not overcome an inspired England side. More than 94,000 England fans did their bit as well.

Bobby Charlton was to prove the hero of the hour. He was the scorer of both goals, and it was probably the finest game he ever played in an England shirt. After his second goal, several Portuguese players were moved to shake him by the hand by way of congratulation upon a remarkable shot – a fairly unusual event in such an important game. At the end of the 90 minutes, as the great Eusebio left the field in tears, Alf Ramsey permitted

himself a rare smile. England had reached the Final of the World Cup.

West Germany had beaten the USSR 2-1 in their semi-final, with goals from Haller and Beckenbauer. Their team for the final was: Hans Tilkowski, Horst-Dieter Hottges, Willi Schulz, Wolfgang Weber, Karl-Heinz Schnellinger, Franz Beckenbauer, Helmut Haller, Wolfgang Overath, Uwe Seeler, Siegfried Held and Lothar Emmerich. England's unchanged line-up consisted of Gordon Banks, George Cohen, Ray Wilson, Nobby Stiles, Jackie Charlton, Bobby Moore, Alan Ball, Martin Peters, Roger Hunt, Geoff Hurst and Bobby Charlton. Jimmy Greaves was most certainly fit by this time, but Ramsey again decided to stick with Hurst. Had things not gone England's way there can be no doubt that the popular, and the not so popular, press would have had a field day.

But things did go England's way – eventually. On the somewhat damp afternoon of Saturday 30 July 1966 the referee blew his whistle to signal the start of a football match which would never be forgotten by England supporters. The first half was not, however, very inspiring, and it all seemed to be going horribly wrong when, after just 12 minutes of play, Ray Wilson's only error of the game let in Helmut Haller to score.

Had Ramsey got it all wrong? Would his efficient and well organised side in the end prove less efficient and less well organised than the Germans? While these questions, and many others, were no doubt going through the minds of those present, the mood suddenly changed. Bobby Moore and Geoff Hurst changed it, as the latter nodded home his captain's free kick to equalise.

Bobby Charlton was being shackled by a young central defender called Franz Beckenbauer and, even though Martin Peters was having a great game, for a time the teams were locked in a kind of stalemate reminiscent of the Great War. Half-time came and went, and the game, along with the weather, began to improve. Then, after 77 minutes Peters, whom his manager had described as being "ten years ahead of his time", latched onto the ball following a blocked Hurst shot and put England ahead.

The English side had only to hold on for less than a quarter of an hour, and time was running out for the Germans. Conscious of this, they seemed to become a little desperate, and began piling in long-range shots from every angle and distance. This was all to no avail but then, with little more than seconds to go, a goalmouth mêlée, following a hotly-disputed free kick, ended up with Weber bundling the ball home. It looked as though Schnellinger had handled the ball in the build-up, but if the Russian linesman missed it he was later to be forgiven.

The World Cup had been within England's grasp, but now the match was going into extra time. Perhaps Jimmy Greaves should have played after all, but Ramsey was stoical. He raised morale by insisting

• **Above**
Captain Moore and manager Ramsey admire the Jules Rimet Trophy at a post-Final reception.

• Above
Bobby Charlton would remain a midfield mainstay of the England side through to the 1970 World Cup.

• Inset
Pickles, the dog who retrieved the World Cup.

to his players that they had beaten the Germans once, and now they had to do it again. It worked, even though, with the weather becoming increasingly warm, both sides were now looking extremely tired.

Next on the agenda was the most famous (or infamous, if you happen to be German) incident in World Cup football. A shot from Hurst hit the underside of the bar, and came down on, or just behind, the goal-line. The referee was unsure as to whether or not the ball had actually crossed the line, and looked to his linesman for guidance. Like almost everyone else, he was confused by the linesman's response – a distinct shaking of the head. Few people in Wembley on that Saturday afternoon knew that, in Russia, a shaken head usually means 'yes' rather than 'no'. A deathly hush seemed to descend upon the Twin Towers, but when the confusion was sorted out the goal was given.

The debate about that goal has gone on ever since. The film has been analysed by 'experts' time and again, but no firm conclusion has been reached. The balance of probability suggests that the whole of the ball did not in fact cross the line, but Geoff Hurst thought it did and, much more importantly, so did the Russian linesman.

At the end, with West Germany pushing everyone forward in a last-ditch attempt to score another equaliser, Hurst again broke free. Some people were on the pitch, thinking it was all over – and it soon was. Hurst scored, the referee blew his

whistle to signal the game's end, and England really had won the World Cup.

The triumph affected the whole nation. Pickles the dog, who had earlier found the stolen trophy in someone's front garden, almost wagged his tail off. Elderly ladies, who had never watched a football match in their lives, took to dancing in the streets, while drunken motorists leapt from their vehicles to embrace passing policemen who were too busy tossing their helmets into the air to notice. And Alf Ramsey smiled yet again. He knew that England had enjoyed their share of good fortune (playing the entire tournament at home had obviously given them a distinct advantage) but he knew too that his tactics and his coaching had paid off. Within a year, he was knighted.

The difficulty for football managers is that, rather like politicians, their careers often end in failure. Sir Alf Ramsey had a great deal to live up to after the 1966 World Cup success, with England supporters naturally hoping that the performance would be repeated four years later. Unfortunately, it doesn't usually work like that.

In any case, before the next World Cup could be considered, England had to ensure qualification for the 1968 European Nations Cup, now re-named the European Championship. It was decreed that the Home Championship should double as the qualifying competition for British sides, and England's first game was at Windsor Park, Belfast, in October – a little under three months after the World Cup final. Sir Alf probably felt obliged to field his World Cup-winning team against Northern Ireland, and he did. They won 2-0, with goals from Hunt and Peters.

The same line-up was again employed against Wales in November, England winning 5-1 with goals from Hurst (2), both Charlton brothers and a Welsh defender. Some new players were introduced as the months went by, in both the Home/European Championship qualifying matches and friendlies, but for the game against Scotland at Wembley in April 1967, the only change from the World Cup-winning team was that Greaves came in for Hunt. Jackie Charlton and Hurst scored for England, but Scotland gained a famous victory by three goals to two.

England were to earn a 1-1 draw in the return fixture with Scotland in February 1968, but they beat

• **Above**
England line up at Wembley, where failure to defeat Poland in qualifying for the 1974 World Cup Finals was to prove Sir Alf Ramsey's undoing.

Wales and Northern Ireland again, and thus qualified for the European Championship quarter-finals.

The ties were played on a two-legged basis, and England were drawn against Spain. The England team for the first game, at Wembley on 3 April, was: Banks, Knowles, Wilson, Mullery, Jackie Charlton, Moore, Ball, Peters, Summerbee, Hunt and Bobby Charlton. Cyril Knowles was a tall full-back from Tottenham Hotspur, with a penchant for upfield surges. Cries of "Nice one, Cyril" were to be heard for many years at White Hart Lane. Alan Mullery was an excellent wing-half, also from Tottenham, while Mike Summerbee was, remarkably, an old-fashioned outside-right from Manchester City who was to gain eight England caps in all.

England beat Spain by a goal to nil in the first encounter at Wembley, Bobby Charlton doing the damage. There were fears that a single goal was not enough to take to the Bernabeu, but those were to prove ungrounded as, a month later, England ran out 2-1 winners with goals from Martin Peters and Norman Hunter. A hard-tackling defender, Hunter

had replaced Summerbee in the line-up. Brian Labone, a centre-half who had, a few years earlier, joined Everton rather than go to university, had replaced Jackie Charlton, while Keith Newton, a cultured full-back from Blackburn Rovers, was in for Knowles.

England had reached the semi-finals. They played a couple of friendlies, beating Sweden 3-1 and losing to West Germany (was that really a friendly?) 1-0, before they faced Yugoslavia, in Florence, on 5 June. The team for the semi was: Banks, Newton, Wilson, Mullery, Labone, Moore, Ball, Hunt, Hunter, Peters and Bobby Charlton. Yugoslavia had a good side, but they seemed bent on destroying the game. It was a thoroughly bad-tempered affair and Alan Mullery became the first England player ever to be sent off. The world champions were eventually beaten by a goal to nil, and were out of the European Championship.

The World Cup loomed once more, with the finals to be played in Mexico. Altitude was always going to be a problem for the European sides but Sir

Alf, together with the entire population of England, was confident that his team would do well. Substitutes were to be allowed for the first time in the World Cup, and red and yellow cards were also to be employed.

England's first group game was against Romania, and a Geoff Hurst goal was enough to win it. Five days later, Brazil were the opponents, and they proved to be just a little more difficult. The England side – Gordon Banks, Tommy Wright, Terry Cooper, Alan Mullery, Bobby Moore, Brian Labone, Alan Ball, Bobby Charlton (Colin Bell), Francis Lee (Jeff Astle), Martin Peters and Geoff Hurst – did well, but not quite well enough. Bobby Moore played superbly and Gordon Banks made one of the greatest saves in the history of the game when he leapt across his goal to save a header from Pele. In the end, however, it was all to no avail. Astle missed a relatively easy chance to equalise, and England lost 1-0.

England were, however, not yet out of it. A 1-0 win over Czechoslovakia, with Allan Clarke (who had played in place of Hurst) scoring from the spot, meant that they qualified for the quarter-finals – and a match against West Germany. It was to be revenge time for the Germans. Gordon Banks was, apparently, ill and was replaced in goal by Peter Bonetti. Bonetti was an excellent 'keeper, but this was not to be his day, and ever since he has been blamed for two of the goals which knocked England out of the competition.

All went wonderfully at first. England had gone two up, with goals from Mullery and Peters, but the team was visibly tiring as the game progressed. After 68 minutes, a routine shot from Franz Beckenbauer easily beat Bonetti, who went down too late. Eight minutes later, Uwe Seeler headed over the stranded England 'keeper, who this time had come off his line. The game went into extra time, during which Hurst had a 'goal' disallowed, and then Gerd Muller scored what proved to be the winner.

• Above
Banks makes one of the finest saves ever against Pele, Guadalajara, June 1970.

The dream had faded.

For Sir Alf, the writing was now on the dressing-room wall. Even so, his side took part in the 1972 European Championship finals, after heading a qualifying group containing Switzerland, Greece and Malta. It was quarter-final time again, and West Germany were to exact further revenge. The match was played over two legs, the first being at Wembley. Germany scored first but Francis Lee equalised after 77 minutes, only for the Germans to score two late goals to put the tie beyond England's reach. The return leg in Berlin was scoreless, and England were out once more.

The end came for Sir Alf when England failed to qualify for the 1974 World Cup finals. They had many chances to beat Poland in the last qualifying game, but in the end could only manage a 1-1 draw. By this time, Ramsey's tactics were considered to be out of date. The 'total football' played by Germany and Holland was proving far more effective, and thus Sir Alf was sacked shortly after the Poland game. Many felt that he had been badly treated as his teams had won 69 out of 113 internationals, losing only 17.

And he had won the World Cup.

Total Football

Chapter FIVE

5

No-one knows which worker it was who took a football out of the British Isles for the first time and opened up the game overseas but the pace of development around the world was swift. By the turn of the twentieth century, the game was being played in almost every country. So much so that in 1903 talk first turned to setting up a world body to look after the interests of the game.

The rest of the world turned to the English for guidance but was met with silence. Robert Guerin, of the Union of French Sports Clubs, met with Frederick Wall, secretary of the FA, but reported, "His head in his hands, Mr Wall listened to my story. He said he would report back to his council. I waited a few months. I travelled to London once more and had a meeting with the FA president Lord Kinnaird. However, that too was of no avail. Tired of the struggle and recognising that the English, true to tradition, wanted to wait and watch, I undertook to invite delegates myself."

FIFA (the Federation of International Football Associations) thus came into being in Paris on 21 May 1904 and comprised France, Holland, Belgium, Switzerland, Denmark, Sweden and Spain. Although invited, not one of the Home Countries was represented, an isolationist attitude that was to have far-reaching implications for years to come. Not least was the decision that FIFA alone would have responsibility for establishing an international competition – the World Cup.

The only action the FA took was to organise a meeting a year later and pass the following resolution: "That it is desirable that the National Associations of the countries of Europe should associate in an International Union for the promotion and control of the game of association football, each association reserving its own jurisdiction within its own area but co-operating with the other associations. No association shall be eligible for membership until it satisfies the Union that it is the only National Association. The Union may arrange an International competition to which entrance by members shall be optional." (FIFA took the resolution to mean they had been given permission by the English FA to carry on as they were!)

It took a further 26 years before the World Cup came into being but, as football grew in popularity around the world there was talk of club competitions involving the best European sides. In the beginning, British sides would travel to Europe and play friendly matches designed to help establish the game in those countries. In time, the quality of football being played in Spain, Italy and Germany was equal to that being played in Britain. However, the time teams would have to spend travelling to and from these countries made the idea of club competition impractical. All that was to change after World War II.

The establishment of European club competition took giant steps towards becoming reality thanks to the development of air travel – it was now possible to reach almost any part of Europe the same day. Equally, with floodlighting allowing evening matches, these would not interfere with work.

There were to be three football matches that proved the catalyst to establishing European competition. Two of these pivotal games were the national side's disastrous performances against Hungary in 1953-54, while the third came in December 1954 when Wolves (then one of the leading club sides) exacted a revenge of sorts by beating Honved 3-2 in a friendly at Molineux.

According to the newspaper reports the following day, Wolves were now the greatest club side in Europe. While it may have been an audacious claim, it did at least galvanise French newspaper L'Equipe into inviting what they regarded as the top 18 clubs in Europe to a meeting to discuss the formation of a European cup competition (editor Gabriel Hanot was known to favour a league format, but the initial meeting settled on a knockout competition).

English champions Chelsea were one of the 16 clubs that attended the meeting and, on 8 May 1955, the European Champion Clubs Cup (it was originally going to be called the FIFA President's Cup in honour of William Seeldrayers of Belgium) came into being. The only restrictions placed by FIFA were that all entrants had to be officially approved by their national associations (a ruling that was to undo Chelsea), that UEFA be responsible for organising the competition and that the name European Cup could not be used (this being reserved for a possible competition for national sides).

Although drawn against Djurgaarden in the first round, Chelsea did not kick a single ball in anger, for the Football League management committee asked them to reconsider their involvement in the competition lest their participation should lead to a fixture crisis. Chelsea withdrew but their Scottish counterparts Hibernian (who weren't even Scottish

• **Opposite**
Real Madrid captain Zarrago holds up the European Cup after his team's 2-0 victory over Reims in 1959.

• **Above**
Chelsea, the League Champions of 1955 who were dissuaded from competing in Europe.

champions at the time, but were rated by L'Equipe as a better side than Aberdeen!) did take part and met Djurgaarden in the second round on their way to the semi-finals. There was no fixture crisis for Hibernian and they ended up £25,000 in profit after their European adventure.

The first Final, held in Paris, featured French champions Stade De Reims and Spanish giants Real Madrid. Reims had beaten Aarhus, Voros Lobogo and Hibernian on their way to the Final, while Real Madrid had seen off Servette Geneva, Partizan Belgrade (winning 4-0 at home but going down 3-0 in the return) and AC Milan. The Final in Paris was a 38,000 sellout, with most of the crowd looking for a French victory.

They might have got it too, for Reims powered into a two-goal lead in the first half, only for Real to equalise by the half-hour mark. Reims took the lead again just after the break, but with Alfredo Di Stefano in irresistible form (he had a hand in all four Real goals) Real were behind for only five minutes and then took the lead for the first time on 79 minutes. They held on for the remaining 11 minutes to be crowned European champions – it was to be a further five years before they lost the title.

While the European Champion Clubs Cup got off to a majestic start, the same could not be said for the Inter Cities Fairs Cup, also launched amid much fanfare in 1955. Twelve sides were invited to take part (invitations were extended to those cities which staged major trade fairs, hence the name), being divided into four mini Leagues, but two withdrawals before the competition started (Vienna and Cologne) meant that groups A and C only had two teams in them. Despite this, it took three years to get through the group stages, with both English entries (a composite London side and Birmingham City) topping their respective groups and advancing to the semi-finals.

The prospect of an all-English Final was dashed by Barcelona, who beat Birmingham City in the semi-final after a play-off at Basle and then beat London 8-2 on aggregate. The damage was done at Barcelona, where the home side raced to a 6-0 victory. Unlike the European Cup (as the premier club competition became known, despite FIFA's plans for the title), the Inter Cities Fairs Cup was not a success, with the 23 games only producing a £3,500 profit after expenses had been deducted – this sum divided among the 12 competitors!

Real Madrid's victory in the European Cup had not gone unnoticed in England, where Manchester United had won the League and had every intention of competing in Europe in the 1956-57 season. The Football League, however, did not agree and tried to persuade United to withdraw, saying "United's participation was not in the best interests of the League". "Prestige alone demands that the Continental challenge should be met, not avoided," was Matt Busby's retort.

United's great European adventure began in Belgium where they beat Anderlecht 2-0. The return was held at Maine Road (Old Trafford did not yet have floodlights) and a sceptical Manchester City believed no more than 10,000 would bother turning up to watch. In the event, more than 40,000 were treated to a magical display as United trounced Anderlecht 10-0 thanks to Dennis Viollet with four goals plus a Tommy Taylor hat-trick, Billy Whelan (two) and Johnny Berry. The only United forward not to score was David Pegg, although he made five of the goals and, after United had scored their tenth, the rest of the forward line spent the remainder of the match trying to engineer a chance for him.

It was a little tighter in the next round, a 3-2 win over Borussia Dortmund at Maine Road being followed by a goalless draw in Germany. Then it was

off to Bilbao to meet Spanish champions Atletico.

It was snowing heavily as United arrived in the city and their plane was forced to land in a deserted field. After a 5-3 defeat the United players then had to help shovel snow off the runway so that their plane could take off for the return home! United made up the deficit at Maine Road, winning 3-0 on the night and 6-5 on aggregate. Their reward was a return to Spain to face holders Real Madrid, but with United on their way to another League title and the FA Cup Final, talk around Manchester was of a possible treble.

In the event this would have to wait more than four decades, for Real Madrid had a little too much experience for United, winning 3-1 in Madrid and drawing 2-2 at Old Trafford (floodlights having now been installed). Matt Busby commented "A good experienced side will always triumph over a great inexperienced side," but that was the reason why United had accepted the invitation in the first place – in order to get experience.

Real Madrid were fortunate enough to host the Final in 1957, with 124,000 of their fans seeing them triumph 2-0 over Italian side Fiorentina thanks to goals from Di Stefano (from the penalty spot) and Gento.

• Above
Legendary Real Madrid centre-forward Alfredo Di Stefano was a major factor in their early European success.

While United's treble dream died against Madrid (and even the Double eluded them as Aston Villa won the FA Cup Final where Roy McParland "was waiting to bag two goals and one goalkeeper," according to one newspaper report), they did win the League and thus get another tilt at the European Cup. After seeing off Shamrock Rovers and Dukla Prague they faced Red Star Belgrade in the quarter-finals. United won the home leg 2-1 and had a number of scares in the return on 5 February 1958 as they drew 3-3 to book their place in the semi-finals. On the way home, however, the plane stopped at snowbound Munich airport to refuel. It was still snowing as the plane attempted to take off and there were two aborted take offs; after the second one, the players returned to the waiting room and made phone calls.

Many were known to want to stay over in Munich rather than attempt a third take off, but at just after 3.00pm on 6 February the pilot was given permission to depart. This time the plane was unable to get enough height and smashed into a house at the end of the runway, killing 23 passengers. Among the dead were eight of United's first team. Also dead were United's trainer, coach and secretary and eight journalists.

The whole of the footballing world was plunged into mourning for the great United side. In addition to those who died, both Jackie Blanchflower and Johnny Berry's injuries meant they never played again, and it was to take the recovering Matt Busby ten years to build another side capable of winning the European Cup.

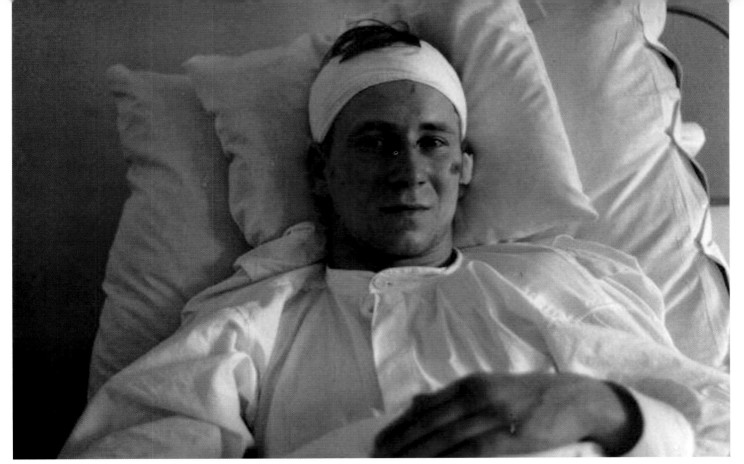

A patched-up United beat AC Milan 2-1 at Old Trafford in the semi-final first leg thanks mainly to emotion but were cruelly exposed in the return as Milan won 4-0. But even Milan could not get the better of Real Madrid, who won 3-2 after extra time in Brussels to retain the trophy for the third time.

When Wolves won the League title UEFA extended an extra invitation to Manchester United to enter the 1958-59 competition as a mark of respect. But the Football League, who had never forgiven United for entering the competition in the first place, refused to allow them to participate, claiming that UEFA's rules would be broken. The fact that UEFA were willing to waive their own rules did not register. Two years on, they had got their revenge on Matt Busby and Manchester United.

Real Madrid were able to extend their grip on the European Cup to five years after beating Stade De Reims in 1959 and then a year later seeing off Eintracht Frankfurt 7-3 in a match that has since been regarded as one of the greatest club fixtures ever played. It was held at Hampden Park and a crowd of more than 127,000 witnessed Real Madrid at their peak. Eintracht were a great side too, as their 12-4 aggregate demolition of Rangers in the semi-final had proved, but Real could boast a line up that included Puskas, Di Stefano and Gento. Alfredo Di Stefano grabbed a hat-trick but was upstaged by Puskas who got four in a match that got a standing ovation at the end.

Real's reign came to an end the following season when, for the first time in five years and after 20 ties, they lost 4-3 on aggregate to fellow Spanish side Barcelona in the first round. Barcelona made it to the Final that year, but any thought of the Cup remaining in Spain disappeared against Benfica, victors by three goals to two.

Benfica retained the trophy the following season too, beating an over-the-hill Real Madrid 5-3 in Amsterdam. England's entrant Spurs had emulated United's previous achievements by reaching the semi-final, but found Benfica in general and their manager Bela Guttmann in particular too great a mountain to climb – they would have their moment of glory in the Cup Winners' Cup.

The success of the European Cup and a revised Inter Cities Fairs Cup (after taking three years to fulfil the first competition and two years the second, the competition had been revised and was now completed in a single season) had prompted calls for an additional European competition for national cup winners. This had been launched in 1960-61 and

• **Above**
Bobby Charlton recovered from his Munich injuries to raise the European Cup a decade later.

Rangers of Scotland had made the Final before being beaten over two legs by Fiorentina. The Italian side reached the Final again the following season before being beaten by Athletico Madrid after a replay.

Atletico also made the Final the following year against Spurs. Dave Mackay was out of the Final with a stomach upset and Danny Blanchflower was still carrying the effects of a knee injury sustained in an earlier round (according to Blanchflower, the choice was either him on one leg or his replacement on two), and for his team talk before the match Bill Nicholson appeared unnerved, talking about the quality of the opposition. After he had left the dressing room, captain Blanchflower took over and addressed the Spurs players one by one, convincing them they had little or nothing to fear.

It worked, too, for Jimmy Greaves and John White put Spurs 2-0 ahead by half time. A penalty brought Athletico back into the game and for twenty minutes they laid siege to the Spurs goal, but the defence held firm and then up at the other end two goals from Terry Dyson and another from Greaves earned Spurs the Cup 5-1. Dyson in particular had a great match, so much so that as he left the field Bobby Smith told him to retire immediately. "Why?" asked Dyson. "Because you'll never play a better game."

Benfica's ending of Real Madrid's reign in the European Cup was to be followed by three years of Italian success. While Benfica and Real had been attack happy and confident that they could score more goals than their opponents, AC and Inter were happy to score one and shut up shop with so-called catenaccio defence. There were other tricks the Italians would use to guarantee success, too, as Bill Shankly

and Liverpool found out to their cost in 1964-65. Drawn against holders Inter in the semi-final, manager Shankly pulled off a stroke in the first leg at Anfield by parading the FA Cup, won a few days previously, just before the match while the Inter players stood around waiting for kick-off. It played on their nerves and they lost 3-0.

But Shankly had an equal in Inter manager Helenio Herrera, who whipped up the San Siro crowd before the second leg, Liverpool being greeted by rockets, smoke bombs and bottles as they walked out. It played on the mind of the referee and a number of dubious decisions (one goal was an indirect free kick while Liverpool had a perfectly good goal disallowed) saw Liverpool tumble out 4-0 on the night and 4-3 on aggregate. Shankly had just had his worst fears about Europeans confirmed.

There was to be British success in Europe that season, however, for West Ham returned to Wembley a year after their FA Cup success to lift the Cup Winners' Cup. Injuries to experienced forwards Peter Brabrook and Johnny Byrne left manager Ron Greenwood with the untried Alan Sealey as his attacking option in the Final against German side Munich 1860, but Sealey scored two goals in as many minutes to ensure West Ham's success and

give skipper Bobby Moore the second of his three trips up the steps to the Royal Box to collect a trophy – a year later, it was to be the World Cup.

The Inter-Cities Fairs Cup was still proving problematic, especially in the 1964-65 season. There were 48 entries, but with no byes in the first round two of six teams left in the quarter-finals got byes into the semi-finals! They were to be joined by Manchester United, enjoying their best European run since the tragedy of 1958. A 3-2 home win over Ferencvaros was followed by a 1-0 defeat, and, since UEFA had not yet implemented the away goals rule, a third, deciding game was necessary. This was won 2-1 by the Hungarians, who then performed even better in the Final, beating Juventus on their home ground to become the first Eastern Bloc side to win a European trophy.

United were back in the European Cup the following season and reached the semi-finals once again. A dazzling performance against Benfica, with United in general and George Best in particular running rings around their opponents (United won 5-1 in Lisbon in one of their greatest ever performances), had convinced Busby that this might be their year. When they avoided Real Madrid in the semi-finals and drew Partizan Belgrade instead, the

• Opposite
Benfica, who ended Real Madrid's European Cup dominance by winning in 1961 and 1962, had a superstar forward in Eusebio.

• Above
Tottenham's Terry Dyson, man of the match in the 1963 Cup Winners' Cup Final, shows off the trophy.

stage was seemingly set for a romantic final. It was not to be, however, for Partizan effectively booked their place with a 2-0 victory in the first leg and, although United reduced the deficit in the second, they could not get a further goal to level the aggregate score.

In the final, Real secured their sixth European Cup with a 2-1 victory, with Francisco Gento having appeared in all six victories and two losing Finals for good measure – his haul of medals will probably never be beaten. Gento retired from the game in 1971, at which point he had also helped Real to 12 League titles.

British sides had stumbled at the semi-final stage six times before finally going one step further in 1966-67. It was not to be Liverpool, England's entry, who were annihilated 7-3 on aggregate in the second round, but Jock Stein's Celtic. Dominant at home (they were to win the Scottish League title nine years in a row), they were novices in Europe by comparison, but Stein could have his players believing they could beat anybody on their day. While their opponents Inter Milan were confined to their training camp in the build-up to the Final in Lisbon, Celtic had open days. And Stein even managed to upstage his rival Helenio Herrera by pinching the bench Herrera had earmarked for himself and refusing to budge.

Herrera had the first laugh, however, when Inter scored and then closed down the game, seemingly having done enough to win the trophy. But Celtic's never-say-die attitude was to have the last laugh, with goals from Tommy Gemmell and Steve Chalmers giving Celtic the victory and cementing the reputation of Jock Stein. "You'll be an immortal," Bill Shankly told him.

Celtic's defence of the trophy didn't get beyond the first round in 1967-68 but in what was the tenth anniversary of the Munich tragedy, there could be only one winner – Manchester United. Their glory bid so nearly came off the rails in the semi-final against Real Madrid, for a 1-0 home victory was followed by a disastrous first half in the return that saw them 3-1 down and completely outplayed. Matt Busby threw caution to the wind in the second half, and goals from David Sadler and Munich survivor Bill Foulkes took them to the Final at Wembley.

There they faced Benfica, complete with Eusebio, Torres and other key Portuguese names. Bobby Charlton gave United the lead, only for Benfica to equalise with 15 minutes remaining. Eusebio might have wrapped it up with barely seconds to go when he burst through the United defence and had only Alex Stepney to beat but, in going for glory and blasting the ball as hard as he could, he hit it too close to Stepney and a point-blank save kept United

• Above
Keeper Ronnie Simpson claims the ball as Celtic beat Inter Milan to Europe's top club prize.

• Inset
Billy McNeill becomes the first Briton to hold the European Cup, 1967.

• **Above**
The 1968 European Cup Final was settled by three extra-time goals for Manchester United against Benfica. George Best's was the first.

in the game. While play raged on, Eusebio still found time to walk up to the keeper and shake his hand!

Their exertions in the 90 minutes had tired Benfica and, with more space to be found, United took control and scored three times in extra time, through George Best (a 25-yard run), birthday boy Brian Kidd and a second from Bobby Charlton. It was Charlton who collected the trophy that meant more than any other to Manchester United, and as he did so Matt Busby cried. "The moment when Bobby took the Cup it cleansed me. It eased the pain of the guilt of going into Europe. It was my justification."

The euphoria surrounding United's victory in the European Cup has always overshadowed Leeds United's triumph in the Fairs Cup that season. Beaten finalists in 1966-67 against Dynamo Zagreb, Leeds had been methodical and clinical in their run to the following year's Final against Ferencvaros. A single strike from Mick Jones in a bad-tempered first leg at Elland Road was enough to earn Leeds their second trophy of the season (they also lifted the League Cup in an equally dour match against Arsenal at Wembley). More to the point, it set up a remarkable run of success for English clubs, Leeds being

followed by victories for Newcastle United, Arsenal and Leeds again in the Fairs Cup. When the competition changed name and format to become the UEFA Cup in 1971, England's grip on the trophy was continued by Spurs and Liverpool.

As luck would have it, the city of Manchester had two entries into the European Cup in 1968-69, Manchester City having won the League title. City would terrify Europe, according to co-manager Malcolm Allison, but they flopped in the first round at Fenerbahce. United meanwhile made it to the semi-final once again, in the season Matt Busby announced his retirement, but couldn't overcome AC Milan to make the Final a perfect swansong for their manager. It was to be another United, Newcastle, who triumphed in Europe that year, winning the Fairs Cup after overcoming Ujpest Dozsa – the last time to date a Newcastle captain has been handed a major trophy!

Even more bizarre was the way the Magpies had qualified for the tournament – UEFA's 'one city, one team' rule had meant that Newcastle were admitted despite finishing tenth in the First Division because the teams above them consisted of three from

London and two from Liverpool. With the two Manchester clubs competing in the European Cup, Liverpool, Leeds and Chelsea in the Fairs Cup and West Bromwich Albion in the Cup Winners' Cup, the fourth Fairs Cup place had gone to Newcastle. They made the most of it.

Manchester City got revenge of sorts by lifting the European Cup Winners' Cup in 1969-70. With Arsenal winning the Fairs Cup and Leeds and Celtic making the semi-finals of the European Cup, there was every possibility all three European trophies were going to end up in the British Isles, possibly even in England. But Celtic had too much experience for Leeds in the European Cup semi-final in a match billed as the Championship of the British Isles, winning home and away for a 3-1 aggregate. Leeds' dream of a League, FA Cup and European Cup treble was to see them end up empty-handed.

Celtic were chasing their own Grand Slam at the time, having already won the Scottish League Cup, being on their way to their 25th League title, and having reached the final of Scottish FA Cup. In the event they lost both finals, Aberdeen getting the benefit of some fortunate decisions in the Scottish FA Cup and Dutch champions Feyenoord making Celtic pay for underestimating them. Although Celtic scored first through Tommy Gemmell, goals from Rinus Israel and, in extra time, Ove Kindvall signalled Holland's first European Cup success.

There was more to follow. While English sides may have dominated the Fairs Cup/UEFA Cup and even the Cup Winners' Cup (Manchester City's success in 1969-70 being followed by a replay victory for Chelsea over Real Madrid a year later), Dutch football was in the ascendant. Feyenoord's European Cup success came as a surprise, not least because they were not even rated the best side in Holland. That honour fell to the Johann Cruyff-inspired Ajax, who confirmed their reputation with a hat-trick of successes in 1971, 1972 and 1973. Their victories were achieved by a largely settled side built around Cruyff, Neeskens and Muhren and employing a free-flowing style that allowed players tactical freedom. This became known as 'total football'.

• Above
Newcastle United's Bobby Moncur raises the Fairs Cup trophy in 1969 under the gaze of goalkeeper Willie McFaul.

• **Above**
Pat Jennings of Tottenham and Eire claims a cross during the first UEFA Cup Final against Wolverhampton Wanderers in 1972.

In contrast, Leeds were still methodical and clinical in equal measure, winning the Fairs Cup on away goals after a 2-2 draw in Turin against Juventus and 1-1 at Elland Road. That was to be the last Fairs Cup Final, for the following season the UEFA Cup was launched. (Leeds, as current holders of the Fairs Cup, met Barcelona, the first winners, to decide who would retain the Cup for good – Leeds lost.)

The first UEFA Cup was very much an English affair, with Tottenham and Wolves contesting the very first all-English Final. Spurs won 3-2 on aggregate, the damage being done in the first leg at Wolves where two goals from Martin Chivers gave the Londoners a 2-1 advantage. Scotland ensured the European Cup Winners' Cup didn't have far to travel, either, Rangers beating Moscow Dynamo 3-2 after being 3-0 up inside 50 minutes. Their good work was undone by their supporters, however, who fought bitter battles with the Spanish police (the match was played in Barcelona) that left one dead and more than 150 injured. Rangers were banned from Europe for two years (later reduced to one on appeal) and there was even talk of the trophy being taken away from them.

There was more trouble the following year, with Leeds this time the victims. Once again in pursuit of a treble, they lost the FA Cup Final against Sunderland, despite being odds-on favourites to win, and fixture congestion undid them in the League, where they slipped to third. The Cup Winners' Cup was an entirely different matter, for there they were undone by a Greek referee and an Italian keeper. AC Milan's keeper Vecchi gave the performance of his career to keep out shot after shot, but he was aided by some curious decisions from Greek referee Christos Michas, denying Leeds two blatant

penalties. The Greek crowd obviously thought so, for they began cheering for Leeds and hurled abuse at the Italian players after their victory.

Liverpool finally got a winning streak going in the UEFA Cup, seeing off holders Spurs in the semi-final and then beating Borussia Moenchengladbach in the Final 3-2 on aggregate. The 3-0 victory in the first leg was harder than it sounded, for the Germans hit the post and missed a penalty (as did Liverpool) and the Reds just about held on in the second leg to complete a unique double – they also won the League title.

Borussia's passage to the Final showed that it was Germany's turn to dominate Europe, and after Ajax's triple success in the European Cup came three successes for Bayern Munich. The first of these was achieved after a replay against Athletico Madrid (semi-final conquerors of Celtic), a 1-1 draw being followed two days later by a 4-0 hammering – Athletico had obviously put their all into the first match and had nothing left to offer. The 1973-74 season, however, was completely overshadowed by the scenes at Feyenoord, where England's run in the UEFA Cup came to an end with Tottenham's 2-0 defeat. More than 200 fans were hurt in rioting by

Spurs fans, which led to them being banned from Europe for two years.

There was more trouble the following year, this time involving Leeds in their European Cup Final clash with Bayern. A disallowed Leeds goal and two possible penalty appeals being turned down were enough to spark widespread fighting, which got more vicious when Bayern scored twice to retain the Cup. Leeds were to be banned from Europe for four years, a sign of things to come for English clubs.

Liverpool repeated their 1972-73 double in 1975-76, winning the League title from QPR and beating Bruges in the Final of the UEFA Cup, although not without a scare or two along the way. More than anything, however, it enabled new Liverpool manager Bob Paisley to show he could more than adequately fill the gap left by Bill Shankly. He proved it beyond doubt the following year (1976-77); pursuing a treble of League, FA Cup and European Cup, it was only the FA Cup that let the club down, Manchester United winning at Wembley. But Paisley knew the European Cup was the real prize, and in Rome against Borussia Moenchengladbach, with Kevin Keegan especially rampant, they powered their way to a 3-1 victory.

• Above
Liverpool manager Bob Paisley and player Ian Callaghan celebrate the club's first European Cup triumph in 1977.

Liverpool's success was to herald a period of domination by the English in European football. Liverpool retained the trophy the following year, a single strike from the new king of Anfield, Kenny Dalglish, at Wembley enough to beat FC Bruges (it was surely ironic that Liverpool's first four European victories should be achieved against the same two sides). Then the mantle passed to Brian Clough's Nottingham Forest, surprise League champions in 1977-78 and victors over Liverpool in the first round of the European Cup in 1978-79.

Despite little or no European pedigree, Forest owed much to their manager's acumen and tactics, especially in overcoming Cologne in the semi-final. A 3-3 draw at the City Ground convinced the Germans they were destined for the Final, but an Ian Bowyer goal in Cologne was enough to earn Forest a Final appearance in Munich. There Clough played his talisman, Trevor Francis, whose £1 million transfer to Forest had come so late in the year he was only eligible for the Final; Francis scored the only goal of the game against Malmo.

Even more surprisingly, Forest retained the trophy the following year in yet more emphatic style, overturning a 1-0 home defeat in the quarter-final against Dynamo Berlin to win on away goals. The Final against SV Hamburg (with a line-up that included former Liverpool hero Kevin Keegan) was

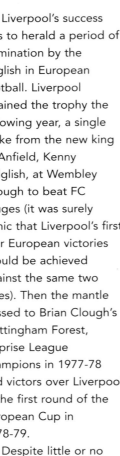

another single-goal victory, the hero John Robertson.

The 1980-81 European Cup Final pitted Real Madrid, in their first Final since 1966, against Liverpool. That the game had changed significantly since Real's dominance was evident in the semi-finals, where the four ties between Liverpool and Bayern Munich and Real and Inter Milan produced only five goals; Liverpool advanced on away goals and Real won 2-1 on aggregate.

It was Liverpool who won on the night, too, Alan

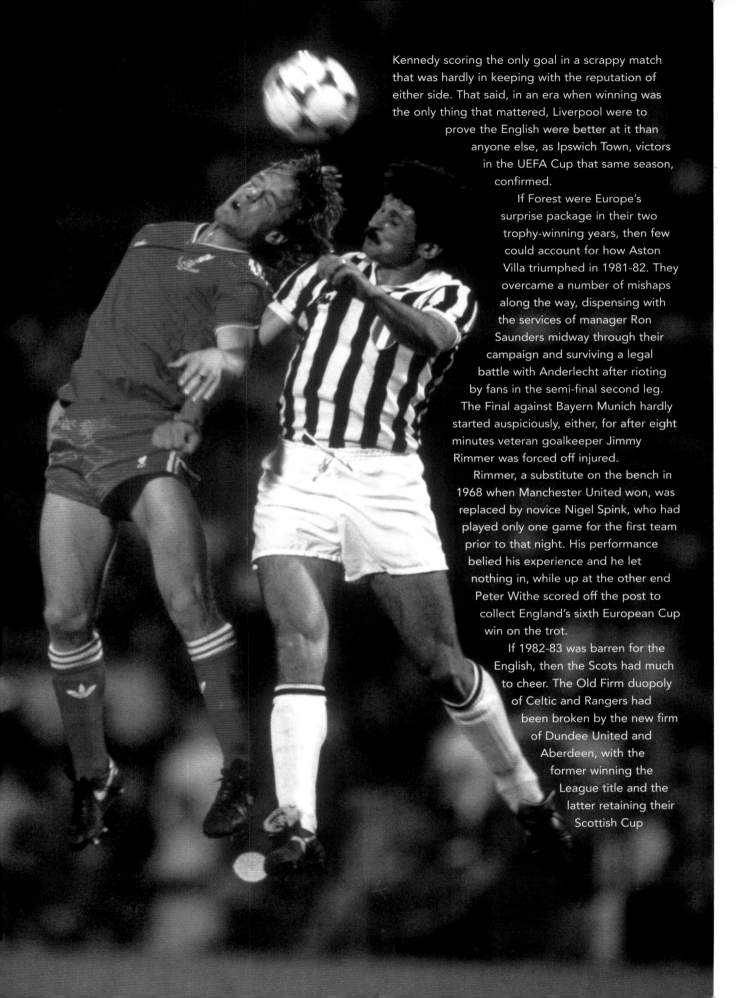

Kennedy scoring the only goal in a scrappy match that was hardly in keeping with the reputation of either side. That said, in an era when winning was the only thing that mattered, Liverpool were to prove the English were better at it than anyone else, as Ipswich Town, victors in the UEFA Cup that same season, confirmed.

If Forest were Europe's surprise package in their two trophy-winning years, then few could account for how Aston Villa triumphed in 1981-82. They overcame a number of mishaps along the way, dispensing with the services of manager Ron Saunders midway through their campaign and surviving a legal battle with Anderlecht after rioting by fans in the semi-final second leg. The Final against Bayern Munich hardly started auspiciously, either, for after eight minutes veteran goalkeeper Jimmy Rimmer was forced off injured.

Rimmer, a substitute on the bench in 1968 when Manchester United won, was replaced by novice Nigel Spink, who had played only one game for the first team prior to that night. His performance belied his experience and he let nothing in, while up at the other end Peter Withe scored off the post to collect England's sixth European Cup win on the trot.

If 1982-83 was barren for the English, then the Scots had much to cheer. The Old Firm duopoly of Celtic and Rangers had been broken by the new firm of Dundee United and Aberdeen, with the former winning the League title and the latter retaining their Scottish Cup

• Above
Paul Walsh (left) of Liverpool and Favero of Juventus pictured during the ill-fated 1985 European Cup Final at the Heysel Stadium in Brussels.

and also winning in Europe. Their Final victory over Real Madrid in the European Cup Winners' Cup was achieved after extra time, where manager Alex Ferguson's rigorous training regime made his men better able to withstand the elements and opposition on a cold night in Sweden than seemingly perennial runners-up Real Madrid.

Liverpool and Spurs triumphed after penalty shoot-outs in the European Cup and UEFA Cup respectively in 1983-84. If Spurs were fortunate winners (it was generally agreed that Anderlecht were slightly the better of the two sides over the two legs), then the same could not be said for Liverpool, who faced Roma on their home ground. Phil Neal gave them the lead, only for Pruzzo to equalise, and with the rest of the game and extra time producing no goals, the stage was set for another penalty shootout.

While the UEFA Cup had made a hero out of Spurs keeper Tony Parks, so the European Cup Final made the reputation of Liverpool's Bruce Grobbelaar, whose antics on the goal-line as he faced the five penalties were enough to force Conti and Graziani to blast over the top. Alan Kennedy's vital strike earned Liverpool their fourth European Cup. It also enabled them to collect a unique treble of League title, League Cup and European Cup in new manager Joe Fagan's debut season.

The only trophy to elude Liverpool that year was the FA Cup, won by fellow Merseysiders Everton.

The following season saw Everton emerge as the new force in English football, snatching the League from their closest rivals, reaching the FA Cup Final and winning the European Cup Winners' Cup, their victories over Bayern Munich in the semis and Rapid Vienna in the Final indicative of their growing prowess in Europe.

How good Everton were or could have been will never be known, for English fans' already tarnished reputation was demolished for good on 29 May 1985. With the domestic game already reeling from the events of the Bradford fire 18 days earlier, which had left 56 people dead, the last thing England needed was trouble on the European front. Unfortunately, the European showpiece between Liverpool and Juventus at the Heysel Stadium in Brussels saw trouble before, during and after the match, left 39 dead and resulted in English clubs being banned from European competition indefinitely.

The game itself, which was only played because the authorities feared further rioting should they abandon it, was won 1-0 by Juventus via a hotly disputed penalty (the tragedy has always overshadowed Juve's accomplishment of becoming the first side to win all three European trophies on offer, following their victories in the UEFA Cup in 1977 and the Cup Winners' Cup in 1984). England's period of domination was at an end.

• **Above**
The European dream goes sour for a Liverpool follower. The club's post-Heysel ban hit them and English football hard.

And how. In the 30 or so years of European competition prior to Heysel, English sides had won the European Cup eight times, the European Cup Winners' Cup five times and the UEFA Cup eight times for a total of 21 European victories, more than any other country. More importantly, the victories were spread around 12 clubs, reflecting the strength in depth of the English game. Since Heysel, English clubs have won the European Cup once, the Cup Winners' Cup three times and the UEFA Cup once – the enforced six-year absence cost the English game more than just the financial rewards of competing in Europe.

While Real Madrid had been the early dominant force in the European Cup, only to be replaced by their Iberian peninsular rivals Benfica, then the Italians, Ajax, Bayern Munich and finally the English, no-one really took over after English clubs were banned. If anything, the European game suffered as much as the English game from the ban; English clubs had understood the mechanics of cup competition, perhaps better than their rivals. Few would have approached the European Cup Final in

1986 as did Steaua Bucharest, who showed no sign of wanting to beat Barcelona in 120 minutes, preferring the lottery of a penalty shootout. In a match Terry Venables' side should have won, they lost 2-0 on penalties.

It was not until 1990 that a club side managed to retain the European Cup again, AC Milan's four-goal hammering of Steaua in 1989 followed by a 1-0 victory over a resurgent Benfica in 1990. The following year it was back to the penalty shootout, Red Star Belgrade winning 5-3 against Marseille after 120 minutes had produced no goals and little entertainment.

That same season (1990-91) had finally seen English clubs re-admitted into European competition, Manchester United making up for lost time with a victory in the European Cup Winners' Cup against Barcelona. It was manager Alex Ferguson's second victory in the competition, following Aberdeen's triumph in 1983, but it was especially welcome for striker Mark Hughes; considered a flop at Barcelona, he was rescued from his Catalan nightmare by Ferguson and repaid him

• **Above**
AC Milan's Gullit shows his pace, beating Dan Petrescu of Steaua Bucherest during the 1989 European Cup Final which Milan won 4-0.

• Above
Barcelona enjoy the
fruits of European
success in 1989 as
Roberto (centre)
celebrates their
victory in the Cup
Winners' Cup Final.

by scoring both United goals in their 2-1 win.

Barcelona had more to cheer the following season, finally winning the European Cup at the third time of asking, beating Sampdoria at Wembley after extra time. Playing in their away kit, they quickly changed after the final whistle to collect the trophy wearing their traditional red and blue stripes. In overcoming Sampdoria, Barcelona emulated Juventus' achievement of having won all three European trophies.

As noted earlier, it was the French who had been largely responsible for the creation of the European Cup back in 1955, but the champagne was to remain on ice for 38 years. In 1993, Marseille, making their second Final appearance, finally got their hands on the trophy, beating AC Milan 1-0 thanks to Basile Boli's header. They were to be subsequently stripped of the title, however, after it was revealed they had bribed an opposition team in the run-up to winning the French title a year before. Technically France still awaits its first European Cup triumph.

AC Milan were back the following year, hammering Barcelona 4-0 in Athens to register their fifth European Cup win, while in the Cup Winners' Cup Arsenal added their second European trophy. The Final against Parma ended "1-0 to the Arsenal", as their fans would sing, thanks to Alan Smith.

There were new plans for the European Cup, however. Since its formation in 1955 it had always been played as a straight knockout competition, the aggregate (or away goals or penalty shootout) winner advancing to the next stage. The bigger clubs in Europe, in particular the Italian and Spanish, wanted guarantees of more games, together with the match and television income it would generate and threatened to break away and organise their own competition if UEFA would not agree.

UEFA finally capitulated, announcing that from 1994-95 the European Cup would be replaced by the UEFA Champions League. Preliminary rounds produced 16 sides who would compete in four mini leagues, guaranteeing each side six games in the first round. The top two in each table advanced to the quarter-finals, where the competition reverted to a knockout format. As luck would have it, Group D produced both finalists, Ajax beating AC Milan 1-0 in the Final having already beaten them home and away in the group stages.

The new competition, with its subsequent amendment of a second round of group matches, has achieved what the big clubs wanted; extra matches that produced extra revenue. Real Madrid were widely reported to be the richest club in Europe, and the money generated by all these extra

with Bayern taking the lead in the Final through Basler on six minutes and still holding it as the game entered injury time. The clocks showed time up and thousands were streaming out of the ground, convinced United's quest had ended in failure, when they won a corner.

Goalkeeper Peter Schmeichel ran the length of the pitch to join this last-ditch attempt at an equaliser, and in the ensuing confusion Teddy Sheringham fired home from short range. Extra time looked assured when United won another corner; this time, Sheringham's flick was met by Solskjaer and they had grabbed victory from the jaws of defeat. Fittingly, it would have been Sir Matt Busby's 90th birthday on the day, 26 May 1999. Like Busby, United manager Alex Ferguson was rewarded with a knighthood, a fitting award for one of the most successful European managers of the modern era.

Bayern would bounce back in 2001, winning on penalties against Valencia, while earlier there had been another German triumph, with Borussia Dortmund beating Juventus 3-1 in 1997. Unfancied Leverkusen might have made it a German hat-trick in 2002, but in the space of a little over a week they lost the German championship, the German League and UEFA Champions League, going down to Real Madrid 2-1 in the Final of the latter.

games was invested in the acquisition of new players, often the best the world had to offer. In recent years, the likes of Zidane, Raul, Ronaldo, Roberto Carlos, Morientes and Solari have been important fixtures of a side that has won three of the last five UEFA Champions Leagues. Their total of nine victories in Europe's top competition, whatever it chooses to call itself, is more than any other club can muster.

In-between Real's domination of the Champions League, there have been victories that other clubs can savour. Chief among these would be Manchester United's win over Bayern Munich in 1999, which enabled them to complete the ultimate treble of FA Premiership, FA Cup and European Cup. The latter competition proved the most difficult to achieve, as you would expect given the quality of opposition,

While there have been lots of extra games for Europe's elite thanks to the new formats, it has been at the expense of everyone else. The European Cup Winners' Cup was scrapped in 1999, Lazio becoming the last ever holders by beating Mallorca 2-1 in the Final at Villa Park. Arsenal might have retained the cup in 1995 but were beaten by an audacious lob from Nayim in the last minute of extra time against Zaragoza, while Chelsea restored English pride with victory in 1998 over Stuttgart.

The format of the UEFA Cup has been redesigned, as the survivors are now joined midway through the competition by the unsuccessful sides from the Champions League. Thus Arsenal started the 1999-2000 season in the Champions League and ended it in the UEFA Cup Final (they lost on penalties). Even the Final is now a single-match affair,

• **Above**
Brown and Van Der Gouw of Manchester United celebrate their club's last-gasp 1999 European Cup win with manager Alex Ferguson.

complete with sudden death or golden goal endings, which saw Liverpool claim their third UEFA Cup in 2001. A 'silver goal' system was introduced in 2003 and came into immediate effect as Porto beat Celtic 3-2 after extra time to win the Final.

The first 40 years or so of European competition saw domination swing from one club to another, from one country to another. To begin with it was a great adventure; that was why Matt Busby defied the Football League. It was an opportunity to test your tactics against the best managerial brains in the world, as Bill Nicholson did against Bela Guttmann. It was teams overcoming a first-leg defeat with displays of all-out attack.

The last seven or eight years have seen the emphasis change. For English clubs, there is a scramble to qualify, with untold riches awaiting those who do and potential bankruptcy facing those, like Leeds United, who don't. The UEFA Cup is seen as little consolation and the scrapping of the Cup Winners' Cup has taken much of the shine off winning the FA Cup.

More recently there has been talk of a single competition to replace both the Champions League and the UEFA Cup. The brainchild of former French international player Michel Platini, it would see some 256 clubs competing in a straight knockout competition. In order to prevent any of the big names going out before the latter stages, sides would be seeded, although there would still be some strong ties in the early rounds. The advantages would be extra places for the traditionally stronger countries – there is talk of England being given 10 or 12 places under Platini's proposal.

The 2004 Final paired Monaco and Porto rather than the expected return of Real Madrid, trophyless for the first time in five years, or 'moneybags' Chelsea. But this underlined the competition's ability to surprise as well as delight; long may it continue to do so.

Chapter
SIX

6

The Premier League, founded in 1992, effectively represented a breakaway from the Football League by its top clubs. With the League a semi-democratic organisation, the bigger clubs felt their smaller brethren were dictating the way the game was run and how the finances were being distributed.

The Football League, formed in 1888 with an initial membership of 12, had, by the late 1980s, grown to 92 clubs. Yet this had been by a process of evolution, rather than revolution. Two further clubs were admitted alongside the original dozen in 1891 and a further two the following year, bringing the numbers up to 16. The same year, 1892, saw the introduction of a Second Division of 12 clubs, bringing the League's size up to 28 clubs in all.

By 1919 the First Division had reached a figure of 22 clubs, a membership it was to retain until 1987. The Second Division's growth kept similar pace, while the introduction of a Third Division in 1920 (enlarged and split into North and South in 1921) had brought the League's strength up to 86 clubs. By 1950 the membership stood at 92, the figure it would retain for four decades.

To fully understand the Premier League founders' motivation in breaking away, it's necessary to examine the way football is financed. It is a subject about which there is, perhaps, more misunderstanding than any other.

For instance, "When the crowd is large at a match there is generally some comment to the effect that the club must be making huge profits, and there is much well-meant advice how the supposed abundance of wealth should be spent."

Those words could be applied to any of the last ten years or so, but they appeared in a history of Tottenham Hotspur published in 1947. The article

went on to reveal that the ground admission to League games in 1945-46 was 10 shillings (50p). "To that was added entertainment tax, introduced to 'all sectors of the entertainment industry' in 1916 in order to raise funds for the war effort. (Like the licensing laws also introduced at the same time, it was retained for decades after the war ended!) The clubs split what was left after the expenses of the game had been met. On a five shilling stand admission the tax was two shillings and six pence, and the clubs had the same amount to divide between them."

This isn't strictly true, for a few years after its formation the Football League settled on an entirely new method of funding itself, taking a small portion (four per cent) of every gate, leaving the two clubs to divide what was left after expenses had been extracted.

This situation endured some 80 or so years. It is worth noting that in the 47 seasons from Spurs' incorporation as a limited liability company in 1898 to the end of the Second World War in 1945, they posted a profit in all but 10 seasons. One assumes the first year's loss was due to expenses incurred in forming a company, after which the club turned a profit in every year up until 1914-15, the year the

First World War broke out and attendances fell alarmingly as spectators went off to enlist in the armed forces.

The depression of the late 1920s and early 1930s, coupled with relegation into the Second Division, saw a loss recorded in four consecutive years. The club recorded their biggest loss in 1939-40, another season in which war was declared, but it is interesting to note that the four years from the 1941-42 season through to 1944-45 saw a profit posted each and every year – this despite the often infrequent nature of organised football at the time, with matches subject to abandonment owing to air raids!

When the war in Europe ended in May 1945, it was felt there was insufficient time to organise proper League football in time for the 1945-46 season, and so the regional Leagues that had been in place for the duration of the war were retained for a further year. Although the football may not have been first class (in the strictest sense of the term), spectators returned to the grounds in search of entertainment after almost six years of war. It was something of a bonanza time for the clubs themselves, all of whom were able to report huge increases in gates and income, so much so that the

• **Opposite**
Alan Shearer's goals helped Blackburn Rovers snatch the Premier League crown in 1995.

• **Above**
The 2003 Premier League title went to Manchester United for the eighth time in 11 years.

119

players threatened to go on strike if their pre-war wages of £8 per week were not raised. They were rewarded with an extra £1 per week, the rise coming in time for further huge increases in gates.

When the Football League resumed in August 1946, more than a million paying customers flooded into grounds up and down the country, despite an unexpected heavy rain falling that day. Indeed, the weather in that first season after the enforced break was to play havoc throughout the year, the 1947 winter being one of the worst ever recorded and forcing the season to stretch into June.

Nothing, however, could dampen the enthusiasm of the spectators, and by the season's end more than 35 million had witnessed the return of League football. The figures kept rising as Britain returned to something resembling normality and, in 1948-49, more than 41 million customers were recorded. In the first four years of League football after the war, more than 157 million people passed through the turnstiles.

As impressive as these figures are, a more interesting figure was revealed at the end of the 1947-48 season. While paying customers had passed the 40 million mark for the first time ever, the BBC

claimed more than one million had witnessed the FA Cup Final between Manchester United and Blackpool on television. Although television had existed before the war, there were insufficient numbers of sets to unduly worry football; after the war the tide turned.

While the subject of televised and radio broadcast matches had been the subject of previous debate, it was not until the Annual General Meeting of the Football League in June 1951 that the matter attracted widespread interest.

The League clubs considered the question of the television and broadcasting commentaries of League games. Sunderland introduced the subject, and gave surprising figures as to the adverse effect on their gates of running commentaries during April. Their view was that running commentaries should be forbidden by the League while matches were in progress but allowed when the games were over.

The majority of clubs were strongly in favour and it was carried on a vote. With regard to televising League games, there was unanimous opinion that it should be banned.

The Spurs handbook for 1951-52 carried the following comments summarising the Tottenham viewpoint: "Since the meeting

of the League, there has been criticism of the action of the clubs in banning running commentaries but the majority of the critics have omitted to mention that commentaries are…only while matches are in progress.

"Efforts have been made by people not concerned with the running of big football to induce the clubs to rescind their broadcasting decision, and appeals were made in newspapers to the Football Association and to the Management Committee of the League to over-ride the decision of the clubs. Of course, the Football Association will not interfere. It permits commentaries on games which are organised by it, but the Football League is master of its own domestic concerns.

"The Management Committee loyally carries out the decisions of the clubs, and certainly will not be in any circumstances jockeyed into a position that would bring them into conflict with the members of the League. In spite of everything that is said by the critics, the clubs know that running commentaries of matches of more than ordinary interest seriously prejudice their gate receipts. Those who argue to the contrary are not acquainted with the facts…

"There is not a club in the League that has not the fullest possible sympathy with hospital patients and the blind, but they point out that big professional organisations in football cannot be run successfully unless there are adequate receipts. Their games are their goods, and they cannot afford to give them away."

While the League meeting had concerned itself with the issue of radio commentaries, in forthcoming years it was to be television that increasingly wished to gain access to the game. Part of a practice match between Arsenal and Arsenal Reserves had been broadcast in 1937, but this was more in the form of an experiment, and this was repeated in 1946 with the televising of an Athenian League (amateur) match between Barnet and Tooting & Mitcham.

A third-round FA Cup match between Charlton Athletic and Blackburn Rovers in the 1946-47 season was the earliest first-class game to be televised live, although there are no reports of the television audience affecting the paying gate. Nor would this be the case for at least a decade or more, not least because television was still very much in its infancy and the number of sets thus a long way off saturation point.

Indeed, it was not until 1966 that television was blamed for adversely affecting a gate; on 5 May that year, the live broadcast of the European Cup Winners' Cup Final between Liverpool and Borussia Dortmund was specifically mentioned as a reason why only 4,554 turned up at Highbury to watch Arsenal face Leeds United, second in the table at the time, in a First Division match. In 1982, the televising of the FA Cup Final replay between Spurs and QPR was similarly held to blame for only 2,315 attending the international between Wales and Northern Ireland, the lowest figure to have witnessed an international fixture since 1892.

• Above
The increasing influence of television and its money fuelled the Premier League launch.

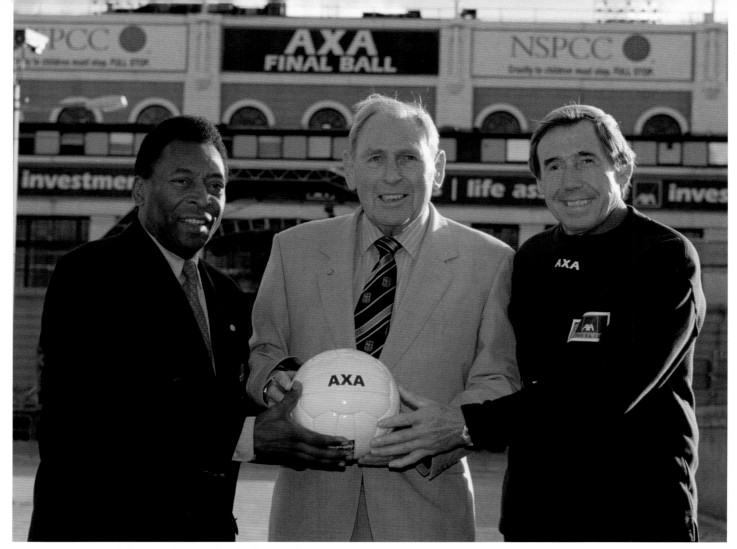

While live televised football was still some way off, football fans unable to get to games did at least start to get a regular fix of the game with the launch of BBC's Match Of The Day in August 1964. Hosted by Kenneth Wolstenholme, the opening show chose the champions Liverpool's clash with Arsenal for its first main feature and was rewarded with a viewing figure of some 75,000, only slightly more than had witnessed the game live at Anfield.

Match Of The Day's viewing figures soon picked up and it became the football programme to watch on a Saturday night. As professional as its presentation undoubtedly was, Independent Television's version screened on a Sunday afternoon was never going to match it and ITV realised that the only way they were going to get similar viewing figures was in poaching the rights from the BBC. In November 1978 they believed they had done so and announced that the following season weekly highlights on a Saturday evening would be appearing on ITV rather than the BBC.

In a deal the papers dubbed 'Snatch Of The Day', ITV announced that they had secured a three-year deal from the Football League, even if some of the clubs themselves could hardly believe what they were hearing. The BBC had no intention of giving up its football flagship without a fight and launched a court action. They won the first round, obtaining an Office of Fair Trading ban on the agreement on the grounds that it broke the rules regarding restrictive practices. In an attempt to satisfy both the BBC and ITV, a deal was brokered whereby the two channels would alternate coverage from season to season during the course of a four-year deal.

While the club chairmen were not in favour as they had no wish to commit themselves to such a long-term deal, the prospect of no televised football whatsoever was enough to get them to sign a £10 million deal and ratify the agreement in June 1979. Not for the last time, however, the television companies had found they held the ultimate bargaining chip – football needed television far more than television needed football.

Despite the success of Match Of The Day it was to be almost 20 years before live football (outside of the FA Cup Final) made a permanent return to British television screens, with Spurs' match against Nottingham Forest on 2 October 1983 the first to be so televised. The programme for the match was hardly in keeping with the fixture's historic nature, commenting: "There will be no records played before today's match or during half-time, as the law does not permit us to broadcast recorded music on a Sunday"!

Overall, however, this was a season of transition and change for the entire game, with the Football League accepting a £1 million a season sponsorship deal with the electrical manufacturers Canon for three years. At the same time, the bigger clubs won an important change in the rules with regard to gate receipts; all clubs now got to keep their home receipts. That the matter was passed by the clubs was surprising, for it was estimated that Coventry City, as an example, would lose some £60,000 a year, but somehow the big guns prevailed.

At the same time, those clubs were also able to bring in similar sweeping changes to other matters concerning the way the game was funded. Central to this was a format of sponsorship from Canon and the Milk Marketing Board (who sponsored the League Cup) that was geared to rewarding the successful teams, complete with a differential in the prize money available between the divisions. Secretary of the Football League at the time was Graham Kelly,

who would later take over a similar role at the Football Association.

While more and more outside money may have been coming into the game, football itself suffered a nightmare decade during the 1980s. Most of the game's problems were caused by the fans themselves – rioting by Millwall fans at Luton during a Cup tie led to the home side banning away supporters altogether for a time, England fans were considered the scourge of Europe after smashing up shops and businesses in Luxembourg, and there were incidents at matches up and down the country.

Two disasters in particular would have a considerable effect on football, culminating in a complete change in the League's makeup. A fire in the main stand at Bradford City midway through their final League match of the season against Lincoln City on 11 May 1985 left 56 people dead. Eighteen days later the European Cup Final between Liverpool and Juventus saw some of the worst scenes ever witnessed as Liverpool fans charged their rivals and 39 spectators were crushed to death after a wall collapsed.

Although the Heysel Stadium in Brussels should never have been chosen for such an important and potentially volatile match and the Belgian police made a catalogue of mistakes before and during the game (no fan was searched on entry, many were admitted while obviously drunk and there was little segregation), this was surely as low as football could get.

• Above
The burnt-out wooden stand at Bradford City's Valley Parade that put safety top of the agenda for all clubs.

The repercussions from both disasters were immense. As a result of the Bradford fire, new regulations were brought in that would effectively close or severely restrict the use of wooden stands. Many of the football stadiums in the country were approaching 100 years old, and many had structures similar to that which had gone up in flames at Valley Parade, Bradford. Football was going to be faced with a huge bill for rebuilding.

UEFA's response to the Heysel disaster was to ban all English clubs from European competition indefinitely, and Liverpool for an extra three years beyond the (unspecified) date when English clubs were admitted back. The loss of revenue for the likes of Liverpool, Manchester United and Spurs, then regulars on the European scene, was immense.

Worse, if that were possible, was to follow. In January 1985 the clubs had rejected a £16 million four-year deal for the televising of League football, believing the television companies could afford and would pay more. Despite warnings from the Football League that the game was being devalued by hooliganism, the clubs refused to change their mind at a further meeting in February, certain television would come back with an improved offer.

It didn't, for in May the BBC and ITV issued a one-month deadline for an agreement to be reached or the offer would be withdrawn. The 1985-86 season kicked off with no television deal in place; when a deal was subsequently reached some months later, it was football that had its cap in its hand, settling for a mere £1.3 million for the rest of the season.

The First Division clubs began to get their own way in April 1986 when the voting structure of the Football League changed to reflect their influence – from now on the Second, Third and Fourth Divisions would have a smaller block vote, and only a two-thirds majority would be needed to effect any change.

Renewed negotiations with the television companies were completed quickly, not least because football needed the income. A two-year agreement worth £6.2 million was reached in June, at much the same time it was announced that the First Division was to shrink to 20 clubs over the next two years. Play-offs, which had been a feature of the Football League when the Second Division kicked off in 1892, were to be re-introduced. For now, all talk of a breakaway Super League had been quietened.

The occasion of the Football League's centenary in 1988-89 should have been a cause for celebration, and much of the season was taken up with special events. There was a match between the League and the Rest of the World (including Argentinean Diego Maradona) and a knockout tournament at Wembley. Unfortunately the 1988-89 season will forever be remembered for the tragic events of 15 April.

The FA Cup semi-final between Liverpool and Nottingham Forest at Hillsborough was a repeat of the previous year's clash. Since that earlier match had passed largely without incident, the authorities, both police and football, believed similar arrangements for the second match would suffice. As it was, fundamental errors made at the first match were repeated at the second, this time with catastrophic consequences.

Although Liverpool had an average attendance of 40,000, they were allocated 24,000 tickets for the semi-final, while Forest, with an average of 17,000, were allocated 30,000. Some ten minutes before kick-off, with more than three thousand Liverpool supporters still trying to gain admission to their allocated Leppings Lane End stand, the police took the decision to open the gates. Perimeter fencing, designed to keep fans off the pitch, also had the effect of keeping trapped fans in place, and in the ensuing panic and crush 96 people were to lose their lives.

After decades of neglect and complacency, football's shortcomings were cruelly exposed. The game had ignored fans' requirements for decades, treating them all as potential hooligans and caging them into pens from which there was little or no escape. Matters at Hillsborough were made worse by poor communication between the police and stewards and a lack of first aid and emergency medical equipment.

In truth, this was a disaster that could have happened at almost any ground in the country. Renovation and modernisation at many had only taken place when legislation (such as that introduced after the Bradford fire) dictated. Football clubs had not been helped over the years by the tax laws. Spending profits on the acquisition of new players did not incur tax liability; improving facilities did. Little wonder grounds had been largely ignored for so many years.

• **Opposite**
Tributes marking the loss of life at Hillsborough, 1989. Standing at top-flight games was on the way out from then onwards.

• **Above**
The scene of the tragedy.

• **Above**
The first televised Premiership game saw Nottingham Forest entertain Liverpool, 1992.

The resulting enquiry into the disaster, which led to the publication of the Taylor Report, was to have far-reaching consequences for the game, not least the removal of all standing areas and a move towards all-seater stadiums. The cost to the game was going to be huge, and for once the cost could not be passed on directly to the supporters (although this would not stop one or two clubs trying).

Almost as soon as the report was published, so the clubs began to backtrack – how were the First Division clubs going to fund such enforced renovation when the game's finances were shrinking? What was needed was more games, so a plan to reduce the size of the First Division to 18 (and possibly even lower) was effectively rescinded. In August 1990, therefore, the clubs agreed to return to a 22-club top division.

That same month the clubs announced they were to sign a television deal with Sky and ITV, with 115 matches to be screened live during the course of the season. This caused bickering between the Football League and Football Association, both of whom believed they ran the game, and prompted a court case between the two organisations. The FA announced in April 1991 that it was to create an 18-team Super League, commencing in the 1992-93 season, further details of which were to be revealed in a forthcoming 'blueprint'. On 14 June, 16 First Division clubs signed a document indicating their intention to join the forthcoming Super League: three did not vote and the remaining three voted against.

Five days later the FA released their 119-page Blueprint For The Future Of Football. Aside from the already well-publicised Premier League, which the FA would run, it also contained details of criteria which would have to met by any club wishing to gain promotion to the League – an all-seater stadium with a minimum capacity of 20,000. The Premier League would contain 22 clubs initially, reducing to 18 as soon as was practical, and the remaining 70 Football League clubs was split into new First, Second and Third Divisions, with 22 in the First Division and 24 in each of the other two.

Since the Premier League was to be financed largely by an influx of television money, there were concessions towards the armchair viewer: there would be live screening of a Premier League match every week, along with every England international. A little over a week later, 15 First Division clubs met at the FA's headquarters in Lancaster Gate and agreed to resign from the Football League.

• **Above**
Rick Parry, the architect of the Premier League, who went on to become Liverpool's chief executive.

The following day, a further five followed suit and, at the FA's summer meeting in Torquay, the remaining two clubs committed themselves to the cause, with newly-elected chairman and spokesman Rick Parry announcing the clubs would either follow the FA's plan or go it alone. The Football League as it had been for over a hundred years, was effectively history from that moment.

On 17 July 1991, the majority of First Division clubs signed a 'founder member document', binding them to the forthcoming Premier League. Although the Second Division clubs had not been consulted over any aspect of the new competition, they were offered an olive branch with the promise of three clubs to be promoted while the Premier League remained at 22 clubs.

The following day, the Football Association successfully applied to have the hearing of the Football League's £9 million damages claim delayed until a court could decide whether the FA's plans for the Premier League were legal.

With the new (and last in its traditional form) Football League season just days away, the game was in danger of imploding. A League management committee meeting ended in farce for with, four of the proposed Premier League clubs ineligible to vote, there weren't enough members to form a quorum! The Third and Fourth Division clubs, who had hardly a voice in any of the discussions, announced they would boycott the FA Cup if they felt their position was being undermined.

In an attempt at mediation, FA Secretary Graham Kelly offered the Football League the opportunity of coming under the FA umbrella and working side by side with the Premier League, an offer that was rejected (Kelly had been secretary to the Football League before taking up his position within the FA!). Other clubs, Sunderland among the most vociferous, tried to persuade the Football League clubs to isolate the Premier League by banning promotion and relegation, but to no avail.

How this was supposed to hinder the new League Sunderland were unable to reveal. If anything, Football League clubs would have been better observing the farce that surrounded their own organisation for, with no management committee, an administrator was appointed by the High Court. Even their own commercial director warned that the Second Division clubs, in particular, risked financial ruin if they did not work with the new Premier League.

Isolation as proposed by Sunderland was never a serious option, and the FA agreed to three up to and three down from the Premier League. The real cause of the bickering, however, was revealed in the Football

League's cash demands from the Premier League; £6 million per year for 50 years by way of compensation! Eventually, after more than five months of wrangling, a compromise was reached, with the FA paying £2 million and the Premier League clubs £1 million for the next five years – £15 million as opposed to the £300 million the League had originally demanded.

The Premier League, with all the legal wrangles out of the way, officially came into being on 23 September 1991. The Football League's Rule 11, which had demanded three-year resignation notices from the clubs, was revoked by 51 votes to 9. The 22-club Premier League would also eventually reduce to 20, although there was no stipulation as to when this might occur. Finally (well, almost), with the FA and Football League now at least back on speaking terms, the FA were officially able to ratify the new League season two months after it had started!

The following month, on 10 October, the Premier League held its first meeting and set up a number of committees to formulate rules and a constitution. This seemed to take over a month and discussions were never fully revealed, but a five-page draft did confirm that there would definitely be 22 founder members, the reduction to 20 clubs being delayed until 1994-95.

While relations between the FA and Football League may have thawed, the Professional Footballers Association was proving a tougher nut to crack. Gordon Taylor threatened a players strike unless they were consulted more by the new League, and won backing from the members to hold such a strike unless the PFA were admitted to negotiations. It was not until January 1992 that Taylor could report back to his members that he was encouraged by "a positive response" from Premier League chairman Sir John Quinton.

Despite this, the PFA would later send ballot papers to all First Division players asking whether they would be prepared to boycott or even strike for live television games. A peace offer from the Premier League offered in March was rejected by Taylor, and a vote of all PFA members gave him support (548 votes to 37) for any action he deemed necessary in the battle, involving the refusal to play in televised matches.

Although the figures in a forthcoming television agreement were not yet public, it was widely believed that this would be a groundbreaking deal and one that the players wanted to get their share of. Finally, on 27 April, the PFA accepted a £1.5 million offer from the Premier League, thus averting any talk of a strike.

• **Opposite**
Ryan Giggs celebrates winning the first Premiership title 1992/3.

• **Above**
PFA supremo Gordon Taylor in conversation with Arsenal's Arsene Wenger.

As the final Football League season as was came to en end, with Leeds United taking the First Division title ahead of a Manchester United side that should have won it, we got a glimpse of the Premier League's promised land. On 18 May the FA signed a new television deal with satellite channel BSkyB and the BBC, collecting £304 million over five years in a deal that guaranteed 60 live matches a season (to be screened on a Sunday afternoon and Monday evening on BSkyB) and highlight programmes on Saturday evening and midweek (on the BBC).

More importantly for the clubs concerned, the television money would be split equally among those who had helped earn it, rather than distributed to all 92 clubs in the 'old-style' League. There would also be payments for staging televised matches, far in excess of the money that had been on offer under previous deals. Then clubs had merely been compensated for any shortfall in their crowd figures and income. In 2003 Fulham collected almost £650,000 for the 'inconvenience' of playing two televised matches in three days.)

ITV launched a court bid to get the deal overturned, thus delaying the backslapping for a further month, but in the meantime secured their own deal with the Football League, paying a minimum of £25 million over four years for exclusive highlights of the League and (then Rumbelows-sponsored) League Cup and live screening of the latter's semi-finals and Final. There would also be a number of unspecified live matches.

While the clubs who were to form the new Premier League readied themselves for the forthcoming launch, the old Football League reinvented itself...by renaming the Second, Third

and Fourth Divisions the new First, Second and Third! Clubs would be rewarded for success on a sliding scale (which borrowed its principle from the Premier League), and there was a return to the 'one club, one vote' rule that had held back the bigger clubs for almost a century.

The size of the Leagues did not alter much either, although Aldershot had been forced to resign during the 1991-92 campaign owing to financial difficulties, the first club to do so midway through a season since Accrington Stanley in 1961-62. Things wouldn't be noticeably different in the Premier League either, although there would now be three substitutes

• Above
Leeds' Lee Chapman celebrates his club's title win in 1992 – the last season before the Premier League.

instead of two, a 15-minute half-time break and referees would wear green.

The 'new, improved' Premier League finally kicked off for most clubs on 15 August 1992, with Nottingham Forest and Liverpool meeting in the first Sunday televised game the following day and QPR and Manchester City clashing in the first Monday-night match a day later.

Although Leeds United had triumphed in the last 92-club Football League season, the ensuing 10 years have seen Manchester United head and shoulders the most successful club, both on and off the pitch. Indeed, they have taken the Premier League title on every occasion bar three since the new competition commenced. Their predominance is very much identified with manager Sir Alex Ferguson, in charge since 1986, who has proved their most successful supremo since the legendary Sir Matt Busby. His achievement of League, FA Cup and European Champions League success in 1998-99 eclipsed even Busby's proud record.

Arsenal have won the title three times under urbane Frenchman Arsene Wenger, who built on foundations laid under George Graham and whose League and Cup Double in 2002 starred such towering continental talents as Bergkamp, Henry and Vieira. Blackburn Rovers, under Kenny Dalglish's management in 1995, are the only other side yet to lift the new trophy, modelled on the European Cup itself, thanks to the goals of Alan Shearer and Chris Sutton.

The Scots had formed their own Premier Division as long ago as 1975 to increase the number of competitive games played by the top-flight teams. A Third Division was introduced in 1994, with all divisions being reduced to 10 in number, but the top teams broke away three years later, in emulation of those south of the border, to negotiate their own TV rights. Promotion and relegation to and from the (currently 12-strong) Scottish Premier League remained, albeit only one club a season and that subject to ground criteria.

• Above
Chris Sutton, seen here playing against Liverpool, was half of Blackburn's title-winning strike force of 1995.

131

In a novel move, the Scottish Premier table split after 33 matches, the top six playing to decide European places and the bottom six to decide relegation. Matters continued to be dominated by Celtic and Rangers, however, to the extent that rumours abounded in the early years of this millennium that they would break away and play in England, initially in the First Division. This was accompanied by attempts by the remaining clubs to get a greater say in the future of the Scottish game, the 'Old Firm' using the power of veto to benefit their own interests.

If there has been one central theme to the English Premier League since its inauguration then it is money. Prize money is offered to clubs on a sliding scale according to their League position at the end of the season. There are 'parachute' payments made to clubs who are relegated at the end of each season, but such are the riches and potential riches that are on offer in the Premier League it has become a holy grail for virtually every Football League club.

As many have found out, reaching the Premier League is significantly easier than staying in it, and the number of clubs who have made an immediate return to the First Division after 12 months in the promised land continues to grow. There is little evidence that this trend will ever be reversed, for many clubs are finding that the cost of maintaining their Premier League status on Football League income makes for an impossible equation.

It is now said there are three mini-Leagues within the Premier League; a top table featuring the likes of Manchester United and Arsenal, who have been rewarded for their consistency in the Premier League with the better part of the prize money on offer and additional income from campaigns in the UEFA Champions League their Premier League position has earned them. They have been joined by big-spending Chelsea.

Then there is the middle table, at which sit the likes of Newcastle United and Liverpool, who would like to join those at the top table but lack the consistency and therefore the funds to make that transition. They also cast cautious eyes over those on the bottom table, usually occupied by those coming up from the First Division and likely to make a speedy return.

Players' union boss Gordon Taylor may well have received continuing mandates to extract a larger share of the television money on offer, but it has been achieved at a high price to his members. As salaries and transfer fees escalated in the UK, many clubs began to look for cheaper alternatives and invariably found them in eastern Europe. With lower fees for players often of better ability than those on offer in the UK, the Premier League began to take on the look of the United Nations.

By the time of the Premier League's 10th anniversary, players from as far afield as Australia, America, Lithuania, Estonia, the Czech Republic, Brazil, France, Nigeria, China, Japan and elsewhere could be found plying their trade in the Premier League. This looks set to continue.

Another trend is the tendency towards club interests over those of the national teams. Club chairmen are not primarily interested in helping the national side, since it is they that pay the players their wages: this has led to continuing battles between the England manager and club bosses over the years. Twenty years ago, having a player picked to represent England (or any other country) was an honour; now it is an inconvenience. Yet the same club managers will happily pay transfer fees for players who regularly represent the likes of Japan, China and Brazil and require additional travelling time to and from international matches.

While the standard of football it is possible to watch in England has undoubtedly improved since the Premier League came into being with talents of the calibre of Cantona, Klinsmann, Zola, Van

Nistelrooy, Desailly and Vieira on display, it has been achieved at a cost. At the time of the abolition of the maximum wage in the 1960s, it was widely held that, since being a footballer was such a short-term occupation, the players owed it to themselves to earn as much out of the game as they could in order to prepare for a life outside the game once their playing days were at an end.

Now, it is claimed that even an average Premier League player only needs a single season's money in order to set himself up for life. Fans, who are being asked to pay season tickets increases of up to 30%, can only look on in disbelief as some players collect £100,000 a week for playing the game. Add to this income from sponsorship and endorsements and several players are earning more than £3 million every year.

Little wonder more and more clubs are falling into debt. Unfortunately, as Leeds United found out to their cost in 2003, the bigger the ambition the bigger the bill, the bigger the headache the bigger the pill. While, for a few, the Premier League has been an unqualified success, for the rest it remains an expensive exercise.

• Above
Manchester United's Eric Cantona, recognised in 2003 as the Premier League's most successful 'import' of its first decade.

persistent injury problems, Seaman continued in quiet yet confident fashion for club and country into the current century.

Only occasionally, as with Ronaldinho's winning goal for Brazil in the 2002 World Cup finals, was Seaman's reign questioned. A move to Manchester City in 2003 saw 'Safe Hands' hang up his gloves for good in mid-season due to injury – a sad end to an illustrious career.

Eric Cantona

Eric Cantona made such a mark at Old Trafford that only David Beckham could hope to occupy his trademark Number 7 shirt. The Frenchman's time in England from 1991-97 proved both eventful and successful, that success beginning when he inspired Leeds to the title in 1992. His shock move across the Pennines for just £1.2 million proved one of the biggest transfer coups of all time. Eric the King spurred United to the inaugural Premier League crown – also their first Championship win in 26 years.

Renowned for his short fuse, Eric let the taunts of a fan get the better of him in the now infamous 'karate kick' incident at Selhurst Park in January 1995. The result was a record ban, leaving Cantona with only his heels to kick as United lost the title to Blackburn and the FA Cup to Everton.

The following season saw him determined to reward the faith of manager Alex Ferguson. Despite his delayed entry into the fray, the Frenchman played the football of his life as he drove United on to record the first ever double Double (League and Cup wins in successive years). He finished the campaign as the club's top scorer with 14 League goals and also grabbed the late winner in an otherwise forgettable FA Cup Final against Liverpool. Yet for all his outstanding displays for United, Cantona found

Premier League Stars

David Seaman

Like his goalkeeping style, which has always been solid and reliable, David Seaman took the steady and unspectacular route to the top. Starting life as an apprentice with Leeds, he looked to Peterborough for first-team football. After a couple of years with Birmingham, he moved to Queens Park Rangers for a £225,000 fee. He received his first England cap against Saudi Arabia in November 1988 while still at Loftus Road, making the trip across the capital to Arsenal the following year for £1.3 million to displace John Lukic who, ironically, would return to Leeds, the club where Seaman had failed to make a first-team appearance.

Seaman would pick up a treasury of medals during his time at Highbury and, despite challenges from the likes of Alex Manninger and Richard Wright, remained the man in charge as 2002-03 came to a close. He was also first choice for England, having swept past Peter Shilton and Chris Woods to take his understanding with centre-back Tony Adams to the national side. And though Adams bowed out with

• Above
David Seaman enjoyed a decade as Arsenal and England's undisputed last line of defence.

himself frozen out of the French national side.

Disappointed in what he saw as a decline in his own standards, Cantona walked away from United in 1997 on a high, having helped steer them to four Premier League titles in five years. Beach football and a film career have since occupied his time, while a return to Old Trafford as Sir Alex Ferguson's successor has also been mooted. Either way, he will never be forgotten. Indeed, in 2003 he was acclaimed the Premier League's top 'import' at a celebration of the competition's first decade.

Jürgen Klinsmann

Having been a World Cup winner in 1990 and enjoyed success with Stuttgart and Inter Milan, mercurial German striker Jürgen Klinsmann was already a superstar when he moved from Monaco to Tottenham Hotspur in 1994. But his arrival helped break down the rather insular attitude of the English game. It helped that he didn't take himself seriously, celebrating goals with a 'dive' similar to those he was accused by some of making at the slightest physical challenge.

A total of 29 goals in his first season helped Klinsmann to Footballer of the Year status in 1995. But the club's failure to qualify for European competition led him to return home to Bayern Munich, much to fans' and critics' disappointment.

After picking up a second UEFA Cup winner's medal with Bayern, he would enjoy a Spurs swansong in 1997. With the club facing relegation, he returned on a short-term basis and scored four goals against Wimbledon to ensure they retained Premier League status.

The skilful Klinsmann retired after representing his country at the 1998 World Cup, moving to Los Angeles and, rather than playing out his last years in lucrative fashion, becoming a student. It would be good to see a former player of his intelligence back in the game at some future point.

Gianfranco Zola

Diminutive (168cm) striker Zola was Diego Maradona's successor at Napoli, and became known in Italy for his deadly accuracy with free-kicks. Arriving at Chelsea from Parma for £4.5 million in November 1996, aged 30, he has since played more than 300 games for the club and has become Chelsea's most popular player ever.

The season after his arrival saw Zola notch the winner in the European Cup Winners' Cup Final, but 1999-2000 proved comparatively ordinary and there was talk of a return to Italy when friend and manager Gianluca Vialli hung up his boots. But Zola retained his place in the first team for the 2000-01 season. He didn't seem to be able to score an ordinary goal,

• Above
German sharpshooter Jürgen Klinsmann enjoyed two spells with Tottenham in the 1990s, impressing friend and foe alike.

with lobs, flicks and backheels all specialities. He also managed to accomplish this with a smile on his face.

Despite losing his place to Eidur Gudjohnsen, he scored some memorable goals in 2001-02 and elected to extend his contract and even take on coaching duties. Yet Zola has retained the ability to turn games and make and take goals, ending the 2002-03 season Chelsea's leading scorer. Honours include FA Cup, League Cup and European Cup Winners' Cup winners' medals, but more important is Zola's legacy to both his club and the Premier League.

Dennis Bergkamp

Skilful Amsterdam-born forward Bergkamp was a product of the Ajax youth system and made his first-team debut for his home-town in December 1986. Between then and leaving for Inter Milan in 1993 he picked up Dutch Championship and Cup medals plus a UEFA Cup medal, finishing domestic leading scorer three times. He made his international debut against Italy in September 1990 and remained a regular for the next decade, playing a significant part in Holland's 1994 World Cup campaign.

After two seasons of struggle with Inter Milan, which nevertheless saw him pick up another UEFA Cup medal, he became Arsenal's record purchase when he was bought for £7.5m from Inter in June

1995. Since then he's played a major role in the Gunners' attempts to wrest domination of the Premiership from Manchester United, though his impact in Europe has been blunted due to a well-documented aversion to flying. He completed the double of PFA Player of the Year and Football Writers' Player of the Year in 1998, when he helped Arsenal to the title. This they followed with the Double in 2001-02 and the FA Cup in 2003. Bergkamp extended his contract after the 2004 Premiership win.

• **Above**
Franco Zola celebrates a Chelsea landmark with a typically understated T-shirt message.

• **Inset**
Dennis Bergkamp pre-dated Arsene Wenger's arrival at Highbury, but has been instrumental in Arsenal's success under the Frenchman.

Michael Owen

Michael Owen came to superstardom in his teens, like Pele, Maradona and Best, making a goalscoring debut for Liverpool in 1997 aged 17 years and 143 days. That summer saw him in an England shirt contesting the World Youth (Under-20) Championships in Malaysia. He scored three times as England progressed to the second round, only to be beaten by Argentina. Little did Owen then know he would be facing that country's first team just 12 months later.

When Michael made his full England debut at Wembley against Chile in February 1998, he became the youngest player in the twentieth century to pull on an England shirt: at 18 years and 59 days, he was 124 days younger than the legendary Duncan Edwards. And though he wasn't in the starting line-up when Glenn Hoddle picked his team to play Romania in Toulouse, it took Owen just ten minutes on the pitch to stamp his presence on proceedings with a goal. Argentina saw him score an outstanding individual effort, after which there was no way he could be left out of the team, let alone the squad.

Such a meteoric rise inevitably had to level out, but he's remained England's star striker to this day. European Footballer of the Year in 2001, he has since picked up UEFA and Worthington Cup medals but currently lacks a top-class strike partner at Anfield. For England he remains a talisman, his hat-trick in

England's 5-1 win over Germany in Munich en route to the 2002 World Cup another landmark. Hamstring niggles have dogged him of late but, though the element of surprise was well and truly gone, his ability to retain a Lineker-like calm amid the hustle and bustle of the top flight remains.

Alan Shearer

Rejected as a schoolboy by hometown club Newcastle, Alan Shearer moved to the opposite end of the country to join Southampton. After a title-winning spell at Blackburn, and establishing himself as top scorer in the Euro '96 Finals, England international Shearer came home to Tyneside for a then world record £15 million fee. And despite being absent from the 2002 World Cup through choice, he remains one of the Premier League's top marksmen and in 2003 was acclaimed the competition's top player of its first decade.

Shearer's career glittered right from the start. He became the youngest ever player to score a Football League hat-trick, achieving the feat in a 4-2 win over Arsenal on his full debut when aged only 17 years and 204 days. By the time Blackburn paid £3.6 million to take him to Ewood Park a month before his 22nd birthday he had won three full England caps. He had plundered 22 goals in only 26 League and Cup games when injury cut his season short.

• **Above left**
Liverpool and England's Michael Owen has had much to celebrate since bursting onto the scene in 1998.

• **Above right**
Alan Shearer's whole-hearted efforts have gone unrewarded with honours at club level with Newcastle.

In the next two campaigns Shearer scored 65 goals (including 13 penalties) as Rovers became Premier League Champions in 1995, a year after being runners-up. In his final season with Blackburn, he signed off with an astonishing five hat-tricks and an amazing 31 goals in 35 Premier games. This included the strike in December 1995 which made him the first player to score 100 Premier League goals (he's since passed the 200 mark).

While the richest of continental clubs wanted to sign him, it was Newcastle he wanted to come home to. A serious injury in August 1997 kept him out for six months, but he has since substituted guile for waning pace.

Club honours have proved impossible to come by – consecutive losing FA Cup Finals in 1998 and 1999 the nearest he got to silverware – but Shearer has remained a talisman, and it was his decision to concentrate on domestic football that helped strike partner Craig Bellamy blossom in 2002-03. But Newcastle's fifth-place finish in 2003-04 sparked rumours of a coaching/managerial future for Newcastle's hero.

David Beckham

On 30 June 1998, in France, David Beckham's petulant kick at Argentinean Diego Simeone that resulted in dismissal made England's task of World Cup progress well-nigh impossible. The vitriol whipped up by the press as the side exited the competition was to be repeated at many football grounds over the next season. Would Beckham end up forever regretting one moment of weakness?

Judging by his performances during the following 12 months as Manchester United completed a

corner providing the opportunity for Solskjaer's last-gasp winner.

Beckham's transfer to Real Madrid in 2003 coincided with a rare trophyless season, but he pledged himself to them as 2004-05 season approached.

Thierry Henry

A product of the French National Academy at Clairefontaine, the fleet-footed Henry first came to wider attention by helping Monaco to a UEFA Champions League semi-final in 1998. Still just 20, he finished the season by helping France win the World Cup on home soil.

A move to Serie A with Juventus proved too much too soon, however, and Arsenal rescued him in the summer of 1999.

record-breaking Treble, the answer was not for one moment. And when, just over three years later in October 2001, his free-kick ensured England's passage to the World Cup Finals, his rehabilitation was complete.

Part of the nation's favourite showbiz family, with Spice Girl wife Victoria and sons Romeo and Brooklyn, he is headline news at least once a week. Thankfully, his performances on the right of midfield for club and country are responsible for at least some of them. Accorded the captaincy of England by short-lived national manager Peter Taylor, Beckham has added leadership to his ball skills and is now an automatic choice under Sven-Goran Eriksson. He added the Champions League of 1999 to five Premiership medals, a trademark inswinging

Arsene Wenger saw him as a striker rather than a wide midfielder, and he took to the role like the natural athlete he is. He top-scored again for his country at Euro 2000, which France also won, and his 24 goals won the Premier League's Golden Boot as Arsenal took the Double in 2001. He proved just as prolific a marksman in Europe, scoring seven times in 12 Champions League games, while the 2002-03 season brought a hat-trick in a 3-1 win against AS Roma in Italy.

France could not continue their run of success at the 2002 World Cup, where Henry showed a chink in his temperamental armour by being sent off against Uruguay. He nonetheless went on to shoot Arsenal to the 2004 Premiership title with 30 goals and pick up successive Player of the Year awards for himself.

• **Above**
Thierry Henry, Footballer of the Year 2004 and a towering talent for Arsenal and France – with much more to come.

Football Goes Global

Football in the twenty-first century is a truly global game, thanks to the advance of satellite communications. It's a situation FIFA (Federation Internationale de Football Association, the world governing football body) has sought to foster in recent years by staging the World Cup in new territories.

The first tournament of the current millennium was jointly hosted for the first time by two countries, Japan and South Korea. It followed in the footsteps of the United States eight years earlier, the first time the finals had departed from its traditional strongholds of Europe and South America (the two having previously taken turn and turn about). It was fitting, too, that supposed underdog countries such as the two hosts, Senegal and the USA, should have fared so well in 2002, emphasising the spread of the game and the rising standards from these 'emerging nations'.

The first World Cup trophy (won in perpetuity by Brazil in 1970) bore the name of one Jules Rimet, Honorary President of FIFA between 1921 and 1954. Yet the competition itself was the brainchild of the organisation's secretary Henri Delaunay. He it was who recognised the changes professionalism had made to the face of the game and declared, in 1926, that international football did not belong under the auspices of the all-amateur Olympic Games, "since many countries can no longer be represented by their best players."

Uruguay was the first country to host the event in 1930 – rightly so, being the reigning Olympic champions. They won a hard-fought Final against neighbours and deadly rivals Argentina though, due to the difficulties of long-distance foreign travel in a pre-jet age, just 13 nations (and only four from Europe) took part.

The holders, indeed, failed to travel to Italy to defend the trophy four years later, and again it was the host nation that would triumph, to the delight of dictator Mussolini. All four semi-finalists were European nations, and it was Europe again, in the shape of France, that would host the 1938 finals. (Argentine fans rioted in Buenos Aires when their country was denied the customary 'alternate continent' switch.) Italy retained the title against tough opposition – a record 36 nations having entered – and would, thanks to the outbreak of war, retain the trophy until 1950.

The competition at this point was played on a simple knockout basis, meaning that some nations travelled a long distance for little reward: the Dutch East Indies (later Indonesia), for instance, headed home after a 6-0 footballing lesson from Hungary.

• **Opposite**
Gary Lineker battles Poland's defence in the 1986 World Cup.

• **Above:**
Italy coach Vittorio Pozzo is feted after his team's triumph over the Czechs, 1934.

• **Inset**
Winners Uruguay celebrate a goal in the very first World Cup Final, 1930.

This had changed by 1950 when the finals in Brazil were played in two league-style phases. Uruguay's 2-1 defeat of the hosts proved decisive in deciding the table-toppers, and has since been regarded as the Final even if no one official match was earmarked.

West Germany's 3-2 victory over Hungary in Switzerland in 1954 was remarkable in that the Magyars had beaten their opponents 8-3 in the group stages. No such surprise in Sweden four years later where Brazil, who'd exited to Hungary in the previous tournament in the infamous 'Battle of Berne' (three players dismissed and a dressing-room brawl), thrashed the hosts 5-2, the outstanding Pele (still only 17) scoring twice. Injury in the first game of the Chile '62 finals kept Pele on the sidelines, but his country won nevertheless, brushing Czechoslovakia aside 3-1 in the Final.

Argentina had won the South American competitions of 1978 and 1986, the former of which they also hosted. West Germany had also made the most of home advantage against Holland in 1974, while the Spain World Cup of 1982 saw a Paolo Rossi-inspired Italy conclusively beat the Germans (who would feature in three successive Finals). It seemed, from this pattern, that countries were unlikely to win the trophy outside their own continent: indeed, that had held true from the competition's inception with the single exception of Brazil's Pele-inspired triumph in Sweden in 1958.

England's participation in the World Cup is covered in detail elsewhere, but it is fair to say that until they provided Gary Lineker as six-goal top scorer in Mexico in 1986, they had contributed little to the history of the competition except their win

two decades earlier. The 1986 tournament would, however, go down in history for Diego Maradona's 'Hand of God' goal past Peter Shilton that sent Bobby Robson's side home disappointed. At least they went out to the eventual winners, though beaten Finalists West Germany came back from two goals down before losing 3-2.

The success of Morocco in the 1986 Mexico World Cup, beating Portugal and securing draws with England and Poland, dropped the broadest of hints that Africa would soon be knocking on the world football door. As it happened, that would have to wait until the next century – South Africa will host the 2010 tournament, after Germany – but Cameroon would prove the surprise team of the 1990 competition.

They scored first blood by defeating holders Argentina in the opening game – and though they understandably couldn't maintain that level of form,

• **Above**
Brazil's Pele, in his first World Cup, challenges Sweden keeper Svensson in the 1958 Final. Brazil won 5-2.

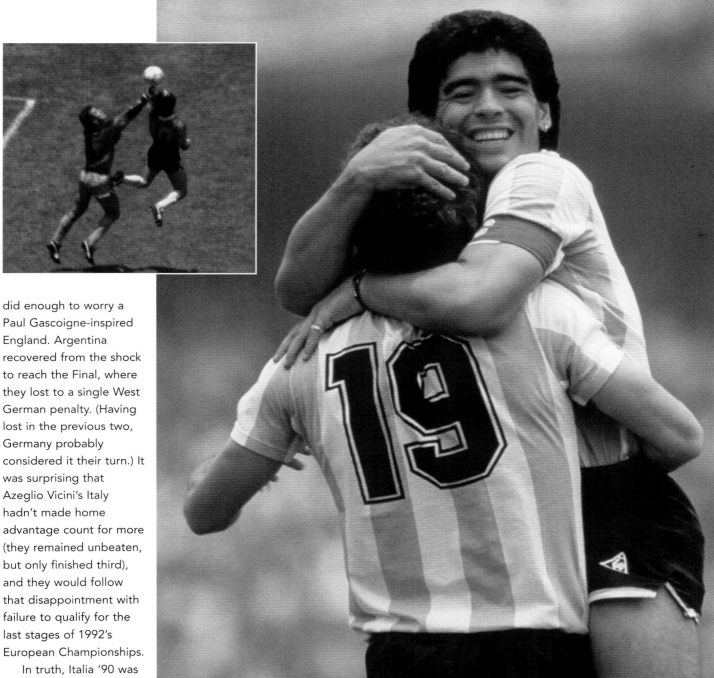

did enough to worry a Paul Gascoigne-inspired England. Argentina recovered from the shock to reach the Final, where they lost to a single West German penalty. (Having lost in the previous two, Germany probably considered it their turn.) It was surprising that Azeglio Vicini's Italy hadn't made home advantage count for more (they remained unbeaten, but only finished third), and they would follow that disappointment with failure to qualify for the last stages of 1992's European Championships.

In truth, Italia '90 was a competition that would be remembered as much for Gascoigne's tears (when, having picked up a booking in the semi-final, he realised his tournament was over) and Scotland's surprise defeat by tiny Costa Rica. Toto Schillaci regained some bruised Italian pride by top-scoring with six.

The grant of the World Cup Finals to the United States in 1994 would not be without controversy. After all, the North American Soccer League, last port of call for many a superannuated European and South American star in the 1970s and 1980s, had sunk without trace and in a welter of lost dollars. Yet that was to ignore the fact that, at grass-roots level, the game was flourishing like no other.

American parents saw it as a safer, less expensive alternative to American (Gridiron) Football and Ice Hockey, while its ability to be played with a minimum of equipment gave it the edge over even baseball and basketball. Add the rise of women's football,

• Above
World Cup joy for Argentina's Diego Maradona after beating West Germany 3-2 in 1986.

• Inset
Maradona's infamous 'Hand Of God' goal beats England's Peter Shilton.

and it was clear that there would be considerable public interest in the tournament. And so it proved, record-breaking crowds witnessing a competition that sparkled until the showpiece Final itself.

That Final featured an Italy managed by Arrigo Sacchi, architect of the all-conquering AC Milan side of the late 1980s. He had reversed the national team's slide to the extent that they were the pre-tournament favourites, but early defeat against Jack Charlton's Eire sounded warning bells. They did, however, make it to the Final this time.

Much was expected of South America and Africa. Of the African nations, Cameroon disappointed in comparison to their 1990 performance, but Nigeria proved the rising stars this time. They headed their group with a goal difference only Brazil could better. Colombia's defeat by the host nation after an opening loss to Romania saw them eliminated. Worse was to come, however, as defender Andres Escobar, whose own goal proved decisive in the second game, was gunned down ten days after returning home. When Bill Shankly made his comment about football being more than a matter of life and death, he surely hadn't bargained for such behaviour…

The highest-profile casualty of the tournament itself, Argentina's Diego Maradona, was a victim of his own making. Playing in his fourth Finals (1986's 'Hand of God' goal still fresh in the memory) and fighting a battle against father time by unfair means, he failed a drug test after his country's second game and was sent home in disgrace. At least he got there: England, under Graham Taylor, had failed to qualify.

The semi-final line-up of Italy, Brazil, Sweden and Bulgaria was hardly the expected quartet – though it was the first two named giants who predictably booked their ticket to the Final itself, each by a single-goal margin. Sadly, the showpiece proved unworthy of an entertaining tournament – a stalemate which neither side looked prepared to lose as the match wore on.

• Opposite
A booked Paul Gascoigne realises his World Cup is over, Italy, 1990.

• Above
The West German team emerges with Colombia at the San Siro Stadium in Milan, 1990.

• Inset
Displaying the trophy, which they'd won for the third time.

The penalty shoot-out will, sadly, be remembered by football historians for the final-kick miss by Roberto Baggio that contributed to Brazil's win. The unfairness of this judgement would have been clear to anyone witnessing his two decisive semi-final strikes against Bulgaria in the Giants Stadium that had taken his team to Los Angeles. Many rated this the tournament's best individual display, but the legacy was heavy strapping that restricted his mobility and effectiveness in the Final itself.

Italy's hugely influential defender Franco Baresi, who was stretchered off against Norway in the group stages and underwent a cartilage operation, made it back for the Final, and played well, but the problem was at the other end. A goalless game ended with a penalty shootout, Baggio's miss ensuring Brazil became the first country to win the World Cup for a fourth time.

France '98 was not only the final tournament of the millennium but, with 32 finalists, the biggest ever. The host nation made theirs the first new name on the trophy for two decades, and few could say they didn't deserve their win. Manager Aime Jacquet would step down after their success, but the team he put together – with names like Barthez, Blanc, Zidane, Henry and Petit – confirmed their class by going on to win the next European Championships.

• **Above**
US player Marcelo Balboa celebrates the host nation's 2-1 win against Colombia in Pasadena's Rose Bowl, June 1994.

Only Nigeria of the African nations survived to grace the last 16, Holland and Croatia making it through to the semi-finals. England's participation under Glenn Hoddle (who controversially elected not to include Gascoigne in his squad) ended in the second round in a game against Argentina notable for Michael Owen's individual goal and David Beckham's dismissal. While third-placed Croatia supplied the top scorer in Davor Suker, it was Brazil's highly-rated hotshot, Ronaldo, who supplied the controversy at the Final itself.

A team sheet was handed in without his name on, then replaced after unspecified goings-on in the changing room. Rumours abounded, speculation suggesting he'd had a fit the night before, but his sponsors Nike had demanded he played. Whatever the truth, he failed to sparkle and Brazil could not profit from the absence of suspended French stopper Laurent Blanc as Zidane (two goals) and Petit wrapped up the coveted trophy.

The success of the 2002 competition jointly hosted in Japan and South Korea was reflected by a Final that pitched the World Cup's traditional giants, Brazil and Germany, against each other. Yet it was the spirited showings of the likes of losing semi-finalists Turkey and South Korea that would linger longer in the memory – plus, of course, Sven-Goran Eriksson's England beating Argentina and leading Brazil for a spell.

• **Above**
Brazilian jubilation as Italy's Roberto Baggio misses the decisive penalty, World Cup Final 1994.

As so often, there was a shock in the opening game when former French colony Senegal put one over on their ex-masters. They passed through to the second round while France, ruing a semi-fit Zidane, went home. Germany were fortunate to beat the United States in the quarter-finals, an American equaliser wrongly disallowed, while plucky Senegal were beaten by a golden goal extra-time strike from Turkey, a country fast emerging as dark horses for the trophy. But the most memorable golden goal came from Korea's Ahn Jung-Hwan against Italy, an achievement which resulted in his Italian club employers giving him his cards!

The Final was a two-goal personal triumph for Ronaldo who put the events of Paris four years earlier firmly behind him to pick up the Golden Boot with eight goals. Germany sorely lacked the suspended Michael Ballack's midfield guile, while usually impeccable keeper Oliver Kahn, at fault for the opener, at least had the player of the tournament trophy as consolation.

• Opposite
In the net! Nigeria's Yekini scores against Bulgaria, 1994.

• Above
US midfielder Claudio Reyna on the ball against Yugoslavia in the 1998 tournament

• Inset
Victorious captain Cafu lifts Brazil's trophy in Yokohama, 2002. It was his country's fifth win overall.

Football Goes Global

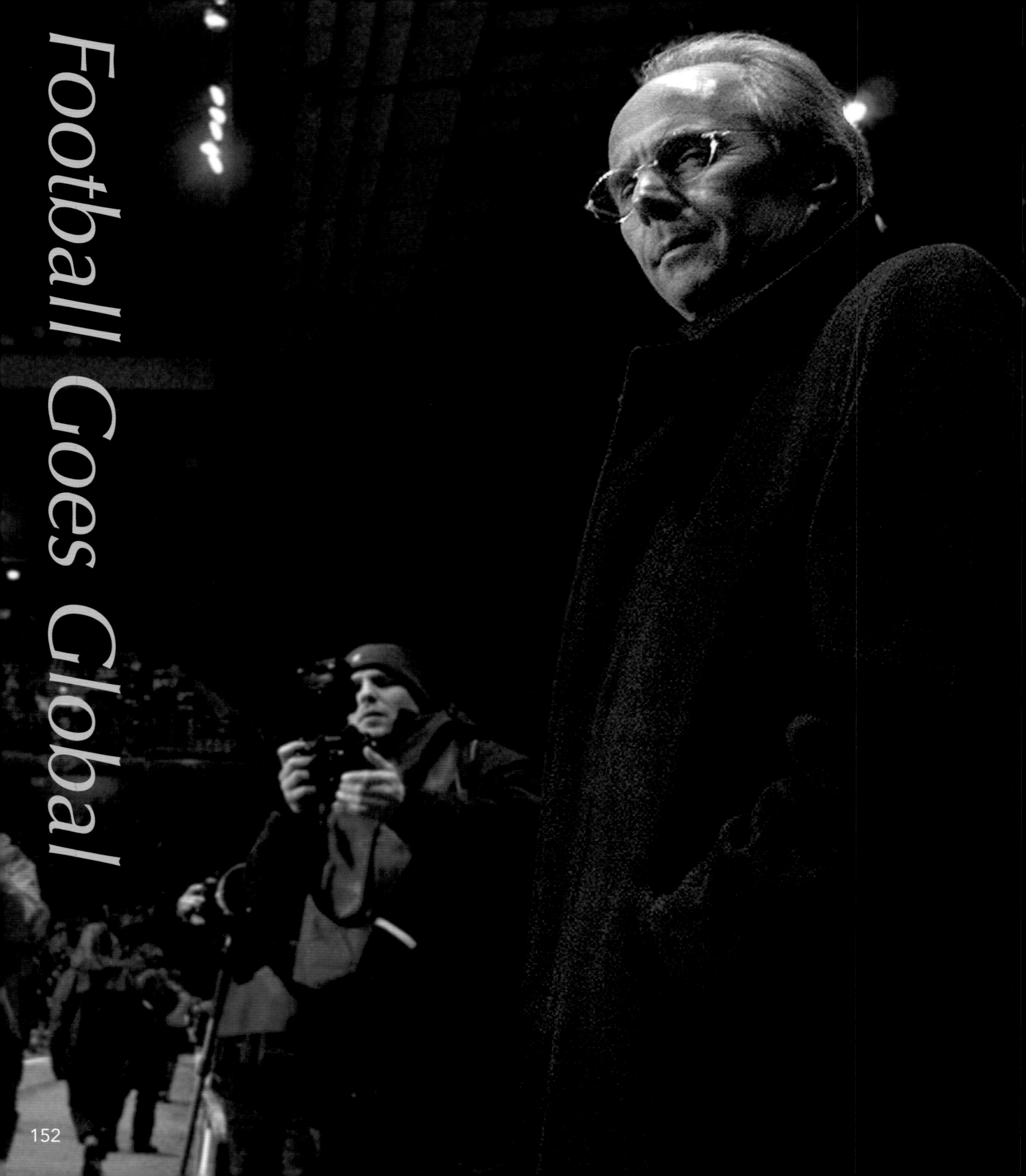

The success of host nations Japan and South Korea was reflected in the European leagues by a slow but steady influx of eastern players. Junichi Inamoto, who'd been signed by Arsenal in 2001 but made few appearances, was snapped up on loan by Fulham. Inamoto, a boy when the J League was created, recalled the thrill of seeing individuals like Gary Lineker, Zico and Dragan Stoikovic at first hand. "They were playing fantastic football in Japan and that made me realise I wanted to be a professional footballer, to play with or against such great players." South Korea's K-League, Asia's oldest soccer league which was founded in 1983, had also featured 'mature' foreign talent like Brazil's Edmilson. With the likes of Sun Jihai (Manchester City) and Toda (Spurs) now also on Premiership show, it seemed the tide was turning.

• Opposite
Sven Goran-Eriksson, the first foreigner to coach England, took them to the quarter-finals of the Japan 2002 World Cup.

• Above
Home-grown hero Junichi Inamoto (left) celebrates scoring against Belgium.

England's display in the 2004 European Championships in Portugal was dominated by teenage striker Wayne Rooney. His two goals in consecutive games that helped bury Switzerland and Croatia went a long way to erasing memories of an opening-match defeat against France that saw the 2000 winners come back from 1-0 down to take the tie thanks to two injury-time strikes from Zidane. When 'Roonaldo' limped off with a broken bone in his right foot in the quarter-final against hosts Portugal England were again one goal up, thanks to Michael Owen. But the concession of yet another late strike brought extra time and, eventually, penalties.

England's poor record in such shoot-outs, dating from Euro 1996, continued as captain David Beckham put the first spot-kick over the bar – and, when Rooney's replacement Darius Vassell saw his shot saved, it was left to Portuguese keeper Ricardo to beat his counterpart David James and send Sven's men home with nothing to show. Many England pundits felt the absence of defensive rock Rio Ferdinand, still absent on a drugs-test technicality, had weakened a back line that conceded six goals in four games, but the wave of flag-bearing patriotism that had made the country feel good about itself was sure to resurface as the 2006 World Cup qualifiers fast approached.

As for Euro 2004, Portugal – who had been both gracious and enthusiastic hosts – saw their dream dashed by a super-efficient Greece side. Otto Rehhagel's men repeated their opening-day group victory, negating the superior skills of Deco, Cristiano Ronaldo and Luis Figo with a fabulous team performance marshalled by man of the tournament Theo Zagorakis and topped by a 57th-minute Charisteas goal.

The Future of Football

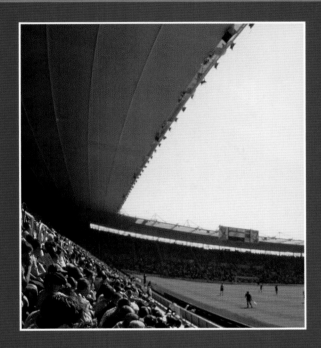

Chapter
EIGHT

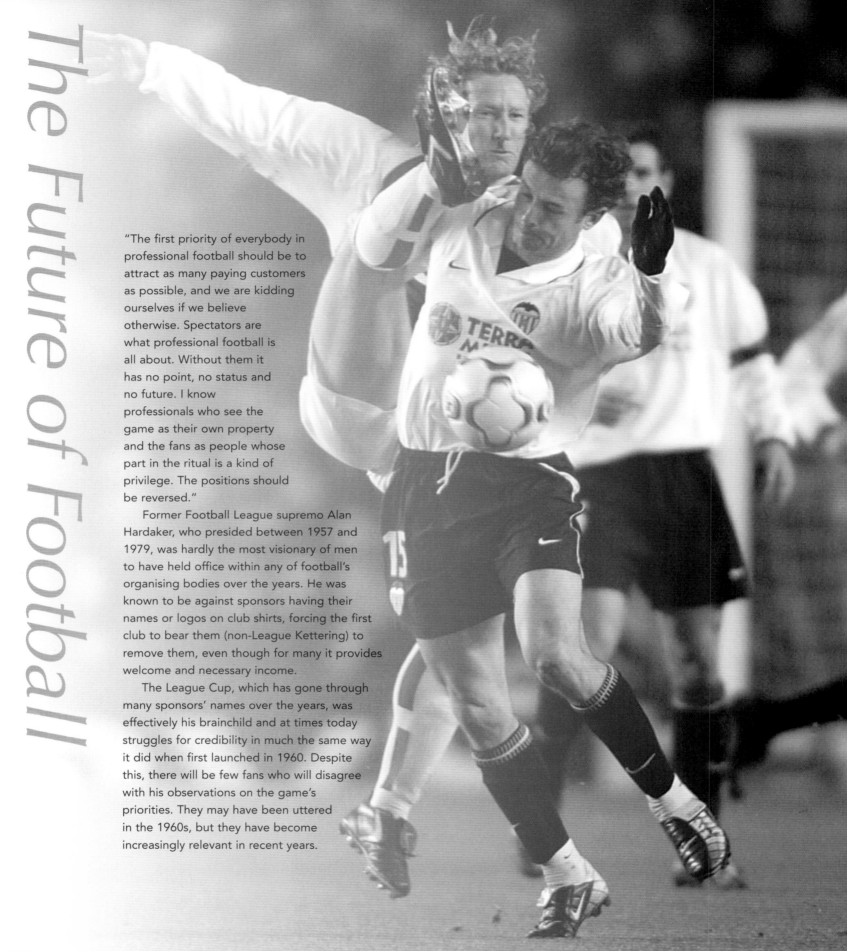

"The first priority of everybody in professional football should be to attract as many paying customers as possible, and we are kidding ourselves if we believe otherwise. Spectators are what professional football is all about. Without them it has no point, no status and no future. I know professionals who see the game as their own property and the fans as people whose part in the ritual is a kind of privilege. The positions should be reversed."

Former Football League supremo Alan Hardaker, who presided between 1957 and 1979, was hardly the most visionary of men to have held office within any of football's organising bodies over the years. He was known to be against sponsors having their names or logos on club shirts, forcing the first club to bear them (non-League Kettering) to remove them, even though for many it provides welcome and necessary income.

The League Cup, which has gone through many sponsors' names over the years, was effectively his brainchild and at times today struggles for credibility in much the same way it did when first launched in 1960. Despite this, there will be few fans who will disagree with his observations on the game's priorities. They may have been uttered in the 1960s, but they have become increasingly relevant in recent years.

Football has become big business. Many of the clubs today are publicly quoted companies with responsibilities to shareholders, investors and the Stock Market to take into consideration. Unfortunately, however, we appear to have arrived at a situation where for many clubs 'success' is measured not in trophies or promotion won but in recording an annual profit, making dividend payments to shareholders and increasing the value of the company. When clubs are signing players based not on their individual abilities but on their ethnic origin in order to 'open up new marketing opportunities', the game's priorities are in question.

Success on the field builds expectation, sometimes to unreasonably high levels. Tottenham's Double-winning side of the early 1960s – featuring the likes of Danny Blanchflower, John White and Dave Mackay – won four trophies in three years. Their counterparts a decade later managed three trophies in a similar spell. Even if it is the considered opinion that no Spurs side before or since can live with the achievements and style of the Double side, three trophies in three years was as good a return as any spectator could hope to see. A further decade on, Spurs were able to deliver three trophies in four years. It is perhaps their lot to deliver to their fans short sustained periods of success a decade apart.

Other clubs enjoyed their own periods of success, sustained or otherwise. Arsenal emulated Spurs' Double achievement with one of their own in 1971. Liverpool repeated the feat in 1986, at a time

• **Opposite**
Arsenal's Ray Parlour in Champions League action, 2002.

• **Above**
Ian Rush, seen in Juventus colours, was a player temporarily lost to English football prior to the Premier League.

when they were the dominant force in the domestic and European game, registering 11 League titles between 1973 and 1990 and topping this with three FA Cups, four League Cups, four European Cups and two UEFA Cups in the same period.

Just prior to the formation of the Premier League, Manchester United began exerting their own domination, and since 1989 have been able to parade eight League titles, four FA Cup triumphs, the European Champions League once, the European Cup Winners' Cup once and the League Cup once in front of their adoring fans at Old Trafford. Even so, Arsenal have closed the gap, winning the domestic Double twice during that period, thus proving that no domination can ever be total.

• Above
Jimmy Greaves left Chelsea for Italy in 1961 in search of financial gain, only to return in a matter of months.

• Inset
John Charles' stay at Juventus was longer and more successful. Nowadays, the Italians come to England.

If Manchester United's achievements on the field are beyond question, their activities off it are often alarming. United probably attracted more attention for becoming the first football club in the world to realise a valuation of £1 billion than almost any of their trophy successes, the European Champions League excepted. Along with Arsenal and Liverpool, Manchester United play a prominent role in the so-called G14 group of clubs. While the richest nations in the world form themselves into G9 to decide and at times dictate world financial matters, so their footballing counterparts in G14 try to influence European football. This has seen proposals for a league involving the biggest European clubs, all of whom would presumably turn their backs on domestic football. At the same time, these clubs are behind the lobbying of FIFA and UEFA to decrease what they see as meaningless international friendlies.

As recently as 20 years ago, British players looking to earn big salaries were usually compelled to join Italian or Spanish clubs. Many top players from that era – Ian Rush, Gary Lineker and Mark Hughes – were lured away in much the same way as their predecessors Jimmy Greaves, John Charles and Gerry Hitchens were swayed by the financial rewards on offer in Italy.

• **Above**
Champions League goal celebrations for Olympiakos in 2002. The competition is now, according to Sir Alex Ferguson, more prestigious than the World Cup itself.

The creation of the Premier League has reduced that traffic, and if anything it is now flowing in the other direction. The Football Association claimed that the 2002 World Cup finals in Japan and South Korea featured more players who plied their trade in the FA Premier League than any other League in the world. A proud boast on the face of it, but the reality is somewhat different. There weren't too many players from either of the two finalists, Brazil and Germany, who could be found in the Premier League. Rather, the bulk of those who play in the Premier League and who performed in Japan and Korea were from the former East European countries and, as noted before, an increasing number from such soccer 'outposts' as Japan and China.

One of the current threats football faces is over-exposure. There will be those, most notably those who don't actually attend games, who are quite comfortable with the amount of televised football that is currently on offer. In what has become the norm, in any given week it is possible to see a Nationwide League match on a Friday evening, a Premier League match at lunchtime on Saturday, two matches on a Sunday (one of which will be pay per view), a fourth Premier League match on a Monday night and possibly three nights of European action. The recent policy of trying to cram as many FA Cup matches into the television schedule as is possible has even seen games being played on a Sunday evening.

This is a punishing schedule even for the most dedicated couch potato, but just recently the players have been giving air to their grievances; since most of the Premier League players have their diets strictly controlled and are required to eat pasta at least three hours before kick-off for energy, those who face a 12.00 lunchtime kick off have to have pasta for breakfast!

It is, of course, the paying customer who is most adversely affected by this chopping and changing of the fixture list. With unreliable public transport available on a Sunday, fans wishing to attend are forced to rely on their own cars, thus adding to the Sunday-night traffic. Those who wish to attend midday kick-offs in the north (in the case of southern-based fans) or south (vice-versa) will often have to contemplate an overnight stay the night before a game in order to guarantee arriving at the ground fresh and on time. Similarly, those who find their clubs away on a Monday night will also incur the cost of an overnight stay and two days' holiday, all for 90 minutes of action!

It is the switch away from a traditional Saturday afternoon kick off at 3.00pm to all manner of days and times that causes fans consternation. It does not affect the players (diets excepted) too much, nor those who make a living out of reporting or televising football, since they all get paid irrespective of the day or time, but the extra expense and trouble does begin to rankle with the most loyal of fans.

The domestic cups have been said to have lost their appeal in recent years, but this seems to be one area where football, aided and abetted by the police, has shot itself in the foot. The needs of the few (ie those competing in Europe) led to the abandonment of replays in the League Cup and, if they get their way again, will also succeed in doing so in the FA Cup. The romantic nature of the FA Cup (and to a lesser extent the League Cup) rests on the ability of a smaller club being able to force a replay at the ground of a bigger club and then complete the upset in their own backyard. Do away with replays and chances are you are doing away with upsets at the same time. And why, in a highly advanced technological era, do the police need ten days' notice of any replay? You can organise and receive police cover for a political rally in less time than that!

• Opposite
Sunderland moved to their impressive new Stadium of Light from Roker Park in 1997.

• Above
Goals from Ruud van Nistelrooy powered Manchester United to a Premier League Championship and the brink of Champions League glory in 2003, until defeated by Real Madrid in the quarter-final.

The collapse of ITV Digital in 2002 resulted in a number of clubs struggling to avoid the bankruptcy courts, usually because they'd already spent the money they believed was going to materialise through the original TV deal. As entertaining as some Nationwide football is, it was never going to have the same kind of appeal as the Premiership. While armchair fans will switch on regularly in order to see if Arsenal or Manchester United can overcome the other in their pursuit of the Premiership, few outside of Wolverhampton will find similar appeal in a Friday-night match against Grimsby, even if one is trying for the play-offs and the other battling against relegation.

Since the matches themselves did not have the required appeal, ITV Digital's sales of the dishes and boxes required to watch the games struggled. Irrespective of the moral or legal arguments that followed Carlton and Granada's decision to put ITV Digital into receivership or liquidation, the spending of money that hadn't yet been received revealed a foolhardy attitude by many clubs.

The safety and security of football's paying customers were objects of the Taylor Report, though in some cases little was done after the installation of seats where terraces once stood. But time waits for no man, and the ever-dilapidating state of Britain's football grounds, most of which were up to a century old, has led to a number of clubs attempting to redevelop their stadium or, in some cases, relocating completely.

This is good news for the spectator with sight lines, facilities, parking and comfort usually radically improved. Unlike in Europe, groundsharing of a purpose-built new stadium was not on the agenda as the new millennium opened, though one top-flight club, Fulham, became tenants of nearby Queens Park Rangers, having forsaken its partially-seated Craven Cottage home due to Premier League regulations. Building a new ground in the capital would not prove as easy, even for multi-millionaire chairman Mohamed Al Fayed, as it had for north-east pair Middlesbrough and Sunderland with their Riverside Stadium (1995) and Stadium of Light (1997).

The success story among new ground owners was Southampton with their Friends Provident St. Mary's Stadium. Opened in 2001, the 32,000-capacity ground was double the capacity of its ageing predecessor, the Dell. As with Bolton's 28,000-seat Reebok Stadium, which opened its doors at the beginning of the 1997-98 season, naming rights have been sold to a sponsor – maybe the latest method of raising revenue.

• **Above**
Bolton chose a new out-of-town stadium to replace dilapidated Burnden Park.

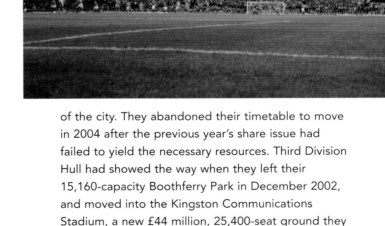

In some cases, however, the process of building a new home has, temporarily at least, proved such a drain on resources as to endanger the financial stability of the club. Leicester City, formerly of Filbert Street, were unfortunate enough to be relegated from the Premier League at the same time as their Walkers Stadium was being completed. Substituting Grimsby for Manchester United and Walsall for Liverpool had an unavoidable effect on attendances (as did the lack of Sky TV revenue) and the club went into administration, though happily success on the field continued and the club was able to recover their Premier League status after just one season.

Manchester City profited from the 2002 Commonwealth Games, for which the 50,000-capacity New Millennium Stadium had been built, and were set to take up residence as tenants to the city council before the 2003-04 season. Neighbours United, who posted the Premier League's record attendance in early 2003, were set to expand Old Trafford from 67,500 to 75,000 by 2006: this will more than double the corporate hospitality area. Newcastle, too, have developed organically to increase St James' Park to a capacity of 52,000.

Everton had aspirations to exchange the 40,000-seat Goodison Park, their home since 1892, for a new 55,000-capacity ground in the King's Dock area of the city. They abandoned their timetable to move in 2004 after the previous year's share issue had failed to yield the necessary resources. Third Division Hull had showed the way when they left their 15,160-capacity Boothferry Park in December 2002, and moved into the Kingston Communications Stadium, a new £44 million, 25,400-seat ground they share with the local Rugby League side.

Hull at least had the assistance of a supportive local council, which funded the project. Other lower-league clubs needed a rich benefactor, as with Wigan and Reading with Dave Whelan and John Madejski respectively. Athletic moved to the 25,000-

• **Above**
Though neighbours Middlesbrough and Sunderland moved, Newcastle United remain at St James' Park.

• **Below**
Bolton's neighbours Manchester United developed their traditional home of Old Trafford to accommodate 67,000.

Work on the new Wembley continued in 2004, eight years after redevelopment was first mooted and two years before it was due to re-open for business.

seat JJB Stadium at the beginning of the 1999-2000 season, 12 months after the Royals opened the similarly sized Madejski Stadium. The club had plans to add an additional 5,000 seats to the East Stand if the need arose. Huddersfield's 24,000-capacity Alfred McAlpine Stadium, opened in 1994, remained one of the more impressive grounds in Divisions Two and Three.

While Arsenal had used Wembley for European matches in seasons past to test out demand, they planned to move into a new 60,000 all-seater stadium at Ashburton Grove in time for the 2004-05 season (a timetable that proved unfeasible due to cash-flow problems). Ironically, many London clubs would have been more than happy to inherit their current 39,000-capacity Highbury ground.

The fiasco that accompanied the planning and building of a new national stadium was symptomatic of the way the game has been run. While Birmingham and Manchester were considered and put forward convincing arguments, only London

could host a World Cup Final or Olympic Games and the 'tendering' process was therefore a red herring.

While the decision to do away with the twin towers caused the most controversy, the funding of Wembley was not far behind. Since the hotel complex at Stamford Bridge very nearly brought Chelsea chairman Ken Bates' own club down, the FA should arguably have learnt from that mistake rather than entertaining plans for a hotel complex as a way of funding the day-to-day running costs of the new stadium.

Meanwhile, as Wembley arose unsteadily from the rubble, Cardiff's Millennium Stadium had temporarily taken its place as venue for the showpiece FA Cup and Worthington Cup (League Cup) Finals. Built in 2000 at a cost of £100 million, it was used by the Welsh International side, but first and foremost by Rugby Union.

With the Football Association in the driving seat thanks to the foundation of the Premier League, it was expected that their chief executive Adam

Crozier would preside over plans for the future of the game. His surprise resignation in late 2002 suggested football had, after all, not got its act together and that the usual anarchy would prevail. So, in his stead, this book concludes with a brief examination of some of the issues and a few possible answers.

Television

While the collapse of ITV Digital was bad enough for the Nationwide clubs so affected, it should also have caused ripples of panic in the boardrooms of the Premiership. The original £350 million deal signed by the FA Premier League and Sky was set at such a high figure because at the time Sky had competition. With ITV Digital also competing for exclusive rights, Sky were forced to go higher than they might otherwise have bid. It will be interesting to see what kind of money is available for a new deal when the current one runs out.

For that reason, perhaps it is time to have a complete overhaul of televised football. While we are still at a stage of demand far exceeding supply as far as match tickets are concerned, why not experiment with making every FA Premier League match available on pay per view, but with all of them kicking off at the same time? Since television crews are at every Premiership match anyway, there should be little or no increase in production costs.

It has been said that the likes of Bury and Stockport suffer a reduction in their gate figures if their matches are up against a live screening of Manchester United or City. If that really is the case (and the die-hard Bury fan is hardly going to miss watching his own team just to watch Manchester United on television), then it should be possible, as in the US, to block off certain parts of the country so that they can't receive the game. Alternatively stagger the matches so that the Nationwide matches kick off at 2.00pm and Premiership games at 4.00pm.

Similar schemes should also be in place for the FA Cup, with all matches kicking off at the same time on a Saturday, pay per view being available for those who want to watch but can't attend.

• **Above**
Television coverage, especially from Sky TV, now dictates when and where Premier League football is played.

165

Domestic Cups

The appeal of the FA Cup has waned since UEFA decided to scrap the European Cup Winners' Cup and only operate two competitions, the Champions League and UEFA Cup. Since the FA Cup is considered the premier knockout competition in England, why not make the reward for winning it entry into the Champions League?

England currently enters four teams in the Champions League, all decided upon by finishing places in the Premier League, and a variable number of entries into the UEFA Cup. The place currently allocated to the team that finishes fourth in the Premier League could go to the FA Cup winners, qualification into the Champions League competition proper being subject to passage through a preliminary round.

Many would say entry into the Champions League should only be achieved by taking a team's performances over a complete season (currently 38 matches) rather than their ability over six cup matches. This is true, but UEFA have arguably forfeited all right to impose such a ruling when a 'champions' League admits teams that finish second, third and fourth in England and a number of other countries.

The FA Cup should also go back to being the type of competition it used to be, with teams

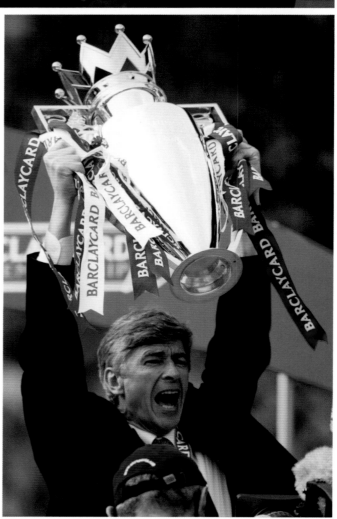

• **Above**
The FA Cup has retained its allure since Terry Venables won it with Tottenham in 1991.

• **Below**
Arsene Wenger with the Premier League trophy, most prized of all domestic silverware.

progressing into the next round only after beating their opponents on the field of play, irrespective of how many replays it requires, rather than the draw taking place while some of the matches were still being played.

There are less compelling arguments for retaining the League Cup. Much was made of the appearance of Liverpool and Manchester United in the 2002-03 Final, the media insisting the competition had come of age and that the big clubs were finally treating it with respect. They conveniently overlooked the number of other clubs who turned out second-string sides yet still expected the fans to pay first-team prices for the privilege. If the winner of the FA Cup got a place in the Champions League, then the League Cup winner should retain their UEFA Cup place. If UEFA won't accept a Champions League place for the FA Cup winners, then the League Cup might as well be scrapped.

The Premier League

The Premier League is the flagship of English football, but there are still many problems that confront it in its second decade. It is still too large in numbers to effectively aid either the national side or even the most successful club sides. With every club

playing a minimum of 40 games at present (38 in the League and a minimum of one each in the two domestic cup competitions), it is inevitable that some matches have to be played in midweek. Take out the weeks that are set aside for European competition, the Saturdays and some midweeks that are lost to internationals and there is a potential for the more successful sides to encounter fixture backlogs.

FIFA has already stated its concern about players being asked to play too many games. Reducing the size of the Premiership to, at most, 18 and preferably 16 clubs would ensure fewer backlogs and hopefully aid the national side. While clubs would be concerned about losing income, a smaller Premier League would have the effect of making every match more of an event. Additional income could be derived from pay per view television, as already mentioned.

The Football League

The collapse of ITV Digital pushed many clubs to the brink of financial ruin, although many of these find themselves there through their own actions, television income merely having delayed the inevitable.

• Above
Middlesbrough manager Steve McClaren and players celebrate the club's first ever major trophy, the 2004 League Cup.

The chances of clubs surviving could be improved if the League were to be restructured. The First Division should be retained as it is, with two clubs being promoted while three come down each year until the Premier League has reached a membership of 18 clubs.

The current Second and Third Divisions should be replaced by three divisions covering the South, Midlands and North. This would reduce the travelling expenses each club would have to incur and also increase the number of local derbies. Additional clubs could be found from the current Conference which, since automatic promotion and relegation between the Third Division and Conference, is the Fourth Division in all but name.

Promotion into the First Division would be automatic for the three regional Second Division champions. Thereafter a further place would be available to the winner of a three-team round robin league between the teams that finished second in their divisions, or a knockout tournament similar to the current play-offs involving the side that finishes third with the best record in any of the three divisions. Automatic promotion and relegation into the feeder leagues would also ensure that the geographical make-up of the new Football League would be retained as far as possible.

It would be up to the individual clubs as to whether they chose to remain full-time or go part-time, but reduced match and travelling expenses must offer them a better chance of surviving than at present. The prospect of Exeter facing a long haul up to Hartlepool for a match that might be postponed (as happened in 2001) would be a thing of the past.

Merchandising

Replica shirts have proved a controversial method of generating merchandising revenue, costing an estimated £5 to manufacture yet retailing at almost £40. In the face of mounting criticism, the FA Premier League passed a ruling limiting clubs to issuing only one new shirt variation (home/away) a year, but many clubs have managed to sidestep or totally ignore the ruling by changing kit manufacturers.

The England shirt of 2003 bucked the trend by being available at a more realistic price – in some cases as low as £25 – so if the national side can do it, there is no reason why individual clubs can't. The more realistic the pricing, the more chance there is that more people will buy them.

Finally, the Premier League should consider taking a leaf out of the books of the basketball and American football associations. It is possible to buy replica kits of the San Antonio Spurs or Miami Dolphins in many countries around the world, so why not dedicated English Premier League shops? The cost of setting these up could be shared by the clubs, spreading the appeal of the Premier League around the world.

Standardisation of prices

It used to be the case that it cost the same to get into Manchester United or Liverpool as it did Watford. The launch of the Premier League has seen clubs raise prices to suit their own ends. Why should clubs charge extra to watch the so called 'gold' or 'platinum' clubs, such as Arsenal, Manchester United or Liverpool, and less for 'standard' clubs such as Middlesbrough and Bolton? After all, we are led to believe the players try just as hard in every fixture.

It should also not cost more to watch Manchester United at Chelsea than it does at Middlesbrough. During the 2002-03 season, it cost £19 to be an away fan at West Bromwich Albion and £21 at both Manchester City and Aston Villa, and a whopping £40 at Chelsea. Manchester United, the most successful club side, charged visitors £25, and even Leeds, with all their financial problems, only asked for £27! Such variations cannot be justified.

Standardisation of prices at a figure of say £30, with increases of no more than the current rate of inflation, would put the game within the reach of the average supporter. There could also be more family tickets on offer, with reduced prices for two or three children, thus ensuring the next generation of supporter gets to experience the magic of the game at first hand.

Supporter Representation

Each club should have supporter representation on their board. Although one or two clubs already have, and others do at least enter into a regular dialogue, it is not nearly enough in any case. There are countless decisions being made which affect the fans that are made with little or no reference as to how it will affect the paying customer.

These include decisions to turn some grounds into no-smoking areas, raising of season ticket prices, turning some areas from season ticket areas to corporate hospitality areas and a host of other, often controversial decisions. While not every decision a board makes is going to be universally accepted by the fans, it is surely better to have reached the decision after consultation.

Relocation

The decision by Wimbledon to relocate to Milton Keynes (after having previously investigated moving to Dublin and then merging with Cardiff) and the ratification by the Football League are worrying signs. If the people who founded Wimbledon in 1889 had been that concerned about setting up their club where there was a catchment area for supporters, they would have moved nearer to London. And

• **Above**
Manchester United's Darren Fletcher hurdles Millwall player-manager Dennis Wise in the 2004 Cup Final. Ticket prices at Wise's former club, Chelsea, are among the Premiership's highest.

while a club moving is still a unique occurence, the lack of argument from the League sets a dangerous precedent.

Any club in the future could put forward the argument that, since their city cannot sustain a top class professional side, they would be better off moving the club 10, 20 or 100 miles up the road. This already happens in America, where most of the major sporting clubs buy a franchise from the governing body. Who is to say that such a scenario could not arise in England?

In moving so far away from their traditional home, Wimbledon have surely forfeited the right to operate under that name. That does not make the situation at the club any better, but to deny the people of Wimbledon, who supported the club as they made their rise through the Football League and to their 1988 FA Cup triumph, the opportunity of watching their club unless they are prepared to make the 100-mile round trip is surely wrong.

Player salaries

At the time the maximum wage was lifted a little more than 40 years ago, professional footballers earned slightly more than the majority of the people who watched them. Even 30 years ago, players earned roughly twice the national average, and then for a much shorter period of time. Now the sky is the limit.

Tottenham's accounts for 2002 revealed the club had an income of £65 million for the year. This was made up of £27.5 million from gate receipts, £22 million from media and broadcasting, £6.7 million from sponsorship, just over £4.5 million on merchandising and £3.3 million from sundry other sources. The biggest expenditure the club faced was salaries, with £32.7 million finding its way into the pockets of the 119 players and coaches, 62 administration and 32 retail staff. While the administration and retail staff undoubtedly do a good job, you can bet they are not earning the lion's

share of the wages! This is a story that is repeated up and down the country, certainly among Premier League clubs.

At present it would seem that the top 5% of players are earning 95% of the salaries that are on offer – and when Manchester United are at home to Liverpool, there are probably more millionaires on the pitch than there are off it! Since football is supposed to be a team game, why should Ruud Van Nistelrooy earn more from Manchester United than his team-mates? Why shouldn't they earn the same basic salary and the same bonus for winning the Premier League or Champions League? Van Nistelrooy should then (as he does) be able to top up his playing salary with image rights payments and his own endorsement and sponsorship deals.

Instead of going to the players, the television money that came into the game could be used to keep admission prices down. If the Premier League passed a rule forbidding clubs from spending more than a set percentage of their income on salaries, it would make chairmen think twice about offering average stars a king's ransom in wages.

Conclusion

As stated at the beginning of this chapter, the most important people in the game are the people who go along every week to watch their side, irrespective of who they happen to support. For too long the needs and desires of these people have been ignored.

• **Above**
Wimbledon FC celebrate their FA Cup win in 1988.

• **Below**
A decade and a half later, an impending move to Milton Keynes sees their temporary home of Selhurst Park all but deserted.

The belief that supporters will turn up every week, irrespective of how their team is doing or how they are going to be received, has taken a bit of a battering in recent years. The 'sold-out' signs don't appear with the same regularity as they did when the Premier League was first launched and there were empty spaces to be seen at many FA Cup matches in recent seasons. Only Manchester United, high-spending Chelsea and Champions Arsenal, who confirmed their move to Ashburton Grove would take place in 2006, seemed immune to fluctuations in demand.

This is obviously an issue that the football authorities need to look at as a matter of some urgency. More than anything, football needs to be proactive rather than reactive, anticipating consumer trends and desires rather than taking them for granted.

Chapter
NINE

9

My team would have to be limited to players that I actually 'saw in the flesh'. No point in my picking Pele, never saw him play outside of the television. With Dunga and Souness holding midfield, the three in front could run riot wherever and whenever they wanted to, leaving the marvellous Dutchman to score at will. Think, too, of the free-kick firepower!

Peter Schmeichel

Schmeichel (born 18 November 1963, Gladsaxe, Denmark) provided Manchester United with a foundation for success after joining them from Brondby for £550,000 in 1991. While at Old Trafford he added many honours to his three Danish Championships and European Championship with his country.

His reach, speed from the line, shot-stopping skills and ability to marshal a defence made him a legend, and it was a surprise when he quit United in 1999 for Sporting Lisbon. Two seasons later he returned to the Premier League first with Aston Villa and then, controversially, United's rivals Manchester City. Though now approaching 40, his large frame – six foot four and 16 stone – made him not only a role model but an imposing figure. He retired in 2003 and quickly established himself as a much in demand figure on radio and television.

Paolo Maldini

A man with a name to live up to, given that father Cesare was a star of the same club, AC Milan, in the 1960s. But Maldini Junior (born 26 June 1968, Milan) showed little fear in establishing himself as a must-pick for club and country after making his first-team debut for Milan in January 1985, at the age of just 16. Originally a left-back in the tradition of Giacinto Facchetti and Antonio Cabrini, he succeeded Baresi in the sweeper's role with calm authority, and captained the national team under his father. Skippered Milan to the European Champions League Final in 2002, their first since '85.

• **Above**
Peter Schmeichel.

• **Below**
Paolo Maldini.

174

Michel Platini

Arguably France's most complete footballer, Platini (born 21 June 1955, Joeuf, France) moved from St Etienne to Juventus in 1982 where his midfield skills and dead-ball wizardry helped him conjure up five years of success. He also became only the second player in history after Johann Cruyff to win a hat-trick of European Footballer of the Year awards.

Having captained France to the 1982 World Cup semi-finals, Platini helped secure the European Championship in 1984, notching nine goals. This was followed by the penalty winner in 1985's European Cup Final against Liverpool, though the memory pales compared with off-field events at Heysel. He proved incredibly prolific both in terms of a midfielder and a player operating in Serie A: 68 goals in 147 Juventus appearances is a major statistic.

In 1986 Platini helped France to third place in the World Cup Finals. Retiring the following year with 72 international caps and many honours to his credit, he would be awarded his country's highest peacetime honour, the Knight of the Legion d'Honneur, and was immediately appointed national coach. Platini relinquished the post after 1992's European Championship but remained active in his country's football administration, playing a major role in their hosting the 1998 World Cup.

Franco Baresi

A superb cool-headed sweeper, Baresi (born 8 May 1960, Travigliato) was able to turn attack into defence with ease for both AC Milan, for whom he played 444 times at top level, and Italy. Unfortunately his last international in the 1994 World Cup Final was marred by a missed penalty in the shootout, but it should be remembered he conquered a mid-competition operation to return to the fray. Six Italian titles, three European Cups, three European Super Cups and two Intercontinental Cups back up fans' claims that he's the greatest Italian defender of all time.

• **Above**
Michel Platini.

• **Below**
Franco Baresi.

Alessandro Costacurta

Another AC Milan stalwart who played alongside Baresi, Donadoni, Maldini and Tassoti. While most of his team-mates moved on in the 1990s, Costacurta (born 24 April 1966, Orago, Italy) held his place to play the best football of his career.

Not only was he one of the mainstays in the Milan defence after an initial season at Monza, but he was in the Italian national squad throughout the mid to late 1990s. He was also billed as one of the unluckiest defenders in Italy as during one cruel year through suspension, he missed a European Cup final, a World Club Cup Final and also the final of the 1994 World Cup when Italy were defeated by Brazil. His San Siro spell continued to the 2003 Champions League Final.

Mauro Tassotti

Tassotti (born 19 January 1960, Rome) was one of the defensive cornerstones of the all-conquering AC Milan side which won the treble of European Cup, European Super Cup and World Club Cup in 1989-90. He combined well on the right side of club and country with midfielder Roberto Donadoni, captaining Milan to European victory against Barcelona in 1994. Named (alongside Franco Baresi) in a Champions League Dream Team selected by UEFA's technical study group to mark the first 10 years of the competition, he now passes on his considerable experience coaching Milan's youth team.

• **Above left**
AC Milan's Alessandro Costacurta.

• **Above right**
Mauro Tassotti shows off the European Cup.

Zinedine Zidane

The all-round talent of Zidane (born 23 June 1972, Marseille) hit the headlines in 1994 when he scored two outstanding goals on his national debut against the Czech Republic. The man who signed for Bordeaux from Cannes in 1992 was at once compared with Platini.

By the summer of 1996 he had done enough for Juventus to pay Bordeaux £3.2 million for his services, and despite a disappointing Euro '96 in England, 'Zizou' recaptured his best form in the black and white stripes, helping Juve to challenge both domestically and in Europe where they reached two Champions League Finals. Successful in steering his national team to the 1998 World Cup and Euro 2000, he struggled against injury in Japan and Korea and couldn't prevent first-group elimination. By this time the 1998 European Footballer of the Year was a Real Madrid player, having joined them in 2001 for a world record £48 million.

Marco Van Basten

Having helped Ajax win the Dutch league in his first full season, 1982-83, Van Basten (born 31 October 1964 in Utrecht, Holland) made his big breakthrough in the 1983-84 season when he scored 28 goals in 26 games. Having played 143 league games and scored 128 goals for Ajax, he signed for AC Milan in 1987-88 but was immediately afflicted by an ankle injury.

The 1988 European Championships gave him the chance to make an improbable comeback, setting up Holland's first goal against Russia in the Final and scoring the second from an impossible angle. He finished top scorer with five. In 1992's European Championship, Holland lost against Denmark, Marco missing a penalty. In club football terms, in-between injuries, he scored an incredible 90 goals in 147 Serie A games (including 25 in 1991-92, a personal record) and had a better than 90 per cent conversion record at penalties.

Van Basten, who retired in 1995, was selected as the best player in Europe in 1988, 1989 and 1992.

• Above left
Zinedine Zidane in Read Madrid's white.

• Above right
The inspirational but injury-plagued Marco Van Basten.

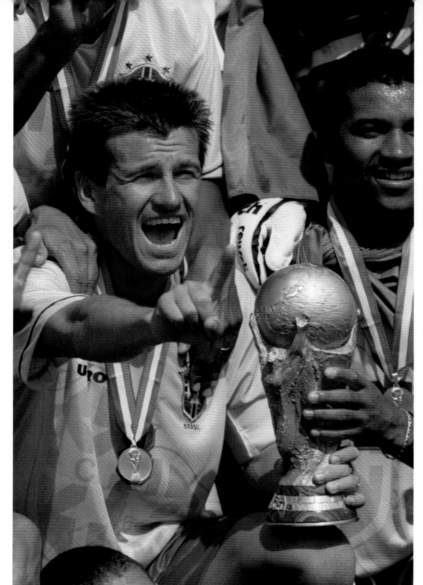

Dunga

Dunga (born Carlos Caetano Bledorn Verri on 31 October 1963, Rio-Grande do Sol, Brazil) began his professional career at Internacional, moving on to Corinthians, Santos and Vasco da Gama. Entering Serie A with Pisa, it was when he moved to Fiorentina that he started to make a name for himself, his club reaching the UEFA Cup Final in 1990.

Subsequent stopping points included Stuttgart and Jubilo Iwata (Japan), where he helped them to the J-League Championship. But it was with the Brazilian national team that he enjoyed his greatest success, participating in three successive World Cup Finals – 1990, 1994 and 1998 – winning in 1994 and coming second four years later.

Graeme Souness

After a false start at Tottenham, Souness (born 6 May 1953, Edinburgh) moved to Middlesbrough in 1973, where he helped them to promotion. Boro fans in 1997 voted him the greatest of all time over Juninho, Pallister et al.

Signed by Bob Paisley for £325,000 in 1978, Souness dominated the centre of the park for Liverpool and captained them to three European Cups, five Championships and four League Cups. Souness, who won 54 Scottish caps, left Anfield for Sampdoria in 1984. He returned to Britain as player-manager of Glasgow Rangers in 1986 but, despite winning the FA Cup in 1992, a subsequent managerial spell at Liverpool proved less successful. Since then he's taken his abrasive style to Galatasaray, Southampton and Blackburn.

• Above left
Dunga shows off the World Cup, the biggest prize in football, USA 1994.

• Above right
Graeme Souness pictured when player-manager at Glasgow Rangers.

Diego Maradonna

The most outrageously gifted player of his generation, Diego Maradona (born 30 October 1960 in Buenos Aires) played in four World Cups, leading Argentina to victory in Mexico in 1986. Club-wise, he left Boca Juniors for Barcelona, then joined Napoli in 1984, helping them win two Championships. Leaving Italy in 1991, he returned home via Seville and retired in 1997 on his 37th birthday.

• **Above**
The unmistakeable Diego Maradona in the colours of his country, Argentina.

English League Champions 1888-2004

SEASON	TEAM	SEASON	TEAM
1888-89	Preston North End	1946-47	Liverpool
1889-90	Preston North End	1947-48	Arsenal
1890-91	Everton	1948-49	Portsmouth
1891-92	Sunderland	1949-50	Portsmouth
1892-93	Sunderland	1950-51	Tottenham Hotspur
1893-94	Aston Villa	1951-52	Manchester United
1894-95	Sunderland	1952-53	Arsenal
1895-96	Aston Villa	1953-54	Wolves
1896-97	Aston Villa	1954-55	Chelsea
1897-98	Sheffield United	1955-56	Manchester United
1898-99	Aston Villa	1956-57	Manchester United
1899-1900	Aston Villa	1957-58	Wolves
1900-01	Liverpool	1958-59	Wolves
1901-02	Sunderland	1959-60	Burnley
1902-03	Sheffield Wednesday	1960-61	Tottenham Hotspur
1903-04	Sheffield Wednesday	1961-62	Ipswich Town
1904-05	Newcastle United	1962-63	Everton
1905-06	Liverpool	1963-64	Liverpool
1906-07	Newcastle United	1964-65	Manchester United
1907-08	Manchester United	1965-66	Liverpool
1908-09	Newcastle United	1966-67	Manchester United
1909-10	Aston Villa	1967-68	Manchester City
1910-11	Manchester United	1968-69	Leeds United
1911-12	Blackburn Rovers	1969-70	Everton
1912-13	Sunderland	1970-71	Arsenal
1913-14	Blackburn Rovers	1971-72	Derby County
1914-15	Everton	1972-73	Liverpool
1920-21	Burnley	1973-74	Leeds United
1921-22	Liverpool	1974-75	Derby County
1922-23	Liverpool	1975-76	Liverpool
1923-24	Huddersfield Town	1976-77	Liverpool
1924-25	Huddersfield Town	1977-78	Nottingham Forest
1925-26	Huddersfield Town	1978-79	Liverpool
1926-27	Newcastle United	1979-80	Liverpool
1927-28	Everton	1980-81	Aston Villa
1928-29	Sheffield Wednesday	1981-82	Liverpool
1929-30	Sheffield Wednesday	1982-83	Liverpool
1930-31	Arsenal	1983-84	Liverpool
1931-32	Everton	1984-85	Everton
1932-33	Arsenal	1985-86	Liverpool
1933-34	Arsenal	1986-87	Everton
1934-35	Arsenal	1987-88	Liverpool
1935-36	Sunderland	1988-89	Arsenal
1936-37	Manchester City	1989-90	Liverpool
1937-38	Arsenal	1990-91	Arsenal
1938-39	Everton	1991-92	Leeds United

• **Left**
Liverpool captain
Ron Yeats holds the
League trophy, 1966.

• **Right**
Arsenal boss George
Graham after
securing the
Championship at
Anfield, 1989.

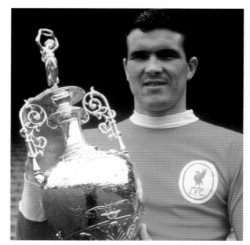

FA Premier League

1992-93	Manchester Utd
1993-94	Manchester Utd
1994-95	Blackburn Rovers
1995-96	Manchester United
1996-97	Manchester United
1997-98	Arsenal
1998-99	Manchester United
1999-00	Manchester United
2000-01	Manchester United
2001-02	Arsenal
2002-03	Manchester United
2003-04	Arsenal

The FA Cup 1872-2004

YEAR	WINNERS	SCORE	RUNNERS-UP
1872	Wanderers	1-0	Royal Engineers
1873	Wanderers	2-0	Oxford University
1874	Oxford University	2-0	Royal Engineers
1875	Royal Engineers	1-1, 2-0	Old Etonians
1876	Wanderers	1-1, 3-0	Old Etonians
1877	Wanderers	2-1 (aet)	Oxford University
1878	Wanderers	3-1	Royal Engineers
1879	Old Etonians	1-0	Clapham Rovers
1880	Clapham Rovers	1-0	Oxford University
1881	Old Carthusians	3-0	Old Etonians
1882	Old Etonians	1-0	Blackburn Rovers
1883	Blackburn Olympic	2-1 (aet)	Old Etonians
1884	Blackburn Rovers	2-1	Queen's Park, Glasgow
1885	Blackburn Rovers	2-0	Queen's Park, Glasgow
1886	Blackburn Rovers	0-0, 2-0	West Bromwich Albion
1887	Aston Villa	2-0	West Bromwich Albion
1888	West Bromwich Albion	2-1	Preston North End
1889	Preston North End	3-0	Wolves
1890	Blackburn Rovers	6-1	Sheffield Wednesday
1891	Blackburn Rovers	3-1	Notts County
1892	West Bromwich Albion	3-0	Aston Villa
1893	Wolves	1-0	Everton
1894	Notts County	4-1	Bolton Wanderers
1895	Aston Villa	1-0	West Bromwich Albion
1896	Sheffield Wednesday	2-1	Wolves
1897	Aston Villa	3-2	Everton
1898	Nottingham Forest	3-1	Derby County
1899	Sheffield United	4-1	Derby County
1900	Bury	4-0	Southampton
1901	Tottenham Hotspur	2-2, 3-1	Sheffield United
1902	Sheffield United	1-1, 2-1	Southampton
1903	Bury	6-0	Derby County
1904	Manchester City	1-0	Bolton Wanderers

YEAR	WINNERS	SCORE	RUNNERS-UP
1905	Aston Villa	2-0	Newcastle United
1906	Everton	1-0	Newcastle United
1907	Sheffield Wednesday	2-1	Everton
1908	Wolves	3-1	Newcastle United
1909	Manchester United	1-0	Bristol City
1910	Newcastle United	1-1, 2-0	Barnsley
1911	Bradford City	0-0, 1-0	Newcastle United
1912	Barnsley	0-0, 1-0 (aet)	West Bromwich Albion
1913	Aston Villa	1-0	Sunderland
1914	Burnley	1-0	Liverpool
1915	Sheffield United	3-0	Chelsea
1920	Aston Villa	1-0 (aet)	Huddersfield Town
1921	Tottenham Hotspur	1-0	Wolves
1922	Huddersfield Town	1-0	Preston North End
1923	Bolton Wanderers	2-0	West Ham United
1924	Newcastle United	2-0	Aston Villa
1925	Sheffield United	1-0	Cardiff City
1926	Bolton Wanderers	1-0	Manchester City
1927	Cardiff City	1-0	Arsenal
1928	Blackburn Rovers	3-1	Huddersfield Town
1929	Bolton Wanderers	2-0	Portsmouth
1930	Arsenal	2-0	Huddersfield Town
1931	West Bromwich Albion	2-1	Birmingham City
1932	Newcastle United	2-1	Arsenal
1933	Everton	3-0	Manchester City
1934	Manchester City	2-1	Portsmouth
1935	Sheffield Wednesday	4-2	West Bromwich Albion
1936	Arsenal	1-0	Sheffield United
1937	Sunderland	3-1	Preston North End
1938	Preston North End	1-0 (aet)	Huddersfield Town
1939	Portsmouth	4-1	Wolves
1946	Derby County	4-1 (aet)	Charlton Athletic

• **Above**

Celebrations as Arsenal clinch the 2004 Premiership on the ground of local rivals Spurs.

YEAR	WINNERS	SCORE	RUNNERS-UP
1947	Charlton Athletic	1-0 (aet)	Burnley
1948	Manchester United	4-2	Blackpool
1949	Wolves	3-1	Leicester City
1950	Arsenal	2-0	Liverpool
1951	Newcastle United	2-0	Blackpool
1952	Newcastle United	1-0	Arsenal
1953	Blackpool	4-3	Bolton Wanderers
1954	West Bromwich Albion	3-2	Preston North End
1955	Newcastle United	3-1	Manchester City
1956	Manchester City	3-1	Birmingham City
1957	Aston Villa	2-1	Manchester United
1958	Bolton Wanderers	2-0	Manchester United
1959	Nottingham Forest	2-1	Luton Town
1960	Wolves	3-0	Blackburn Rovers
1961	Tottenham Hotspur	2-0	Leicester City
1962	Tottenham Hotspur	3-1	Burnley
1963	Manchester United	3-1	Leicester City
1964	West Ham United	3-2	Preston North End
1965	Liverpool	2-1 (aet)	Leeds United
1966	Everton	3-2	Sheffield Wednesday
1967	Tottenham Hotspur	2-1	Chelsea
1968	West Bromwich Albion	1-0 (aet)	Everton
1969	Manchester City	1-0	Leicester City
1970	Chelsea	2-2 (aet), 2-1 (aet)	Leeds United
1971	Arsenal	2-1 (aet)	Liverpool
1972	Leeds United	1-0	Arsenal
1973	Sunderland	1-0	Leeds United
1974	Liverpool	3-0	Newcastle United
1975	West Ham United	2-0	Fulham
1976	Southampton	1-0	Manchester United

YEAR	WINNERS	SCORE	RUNNERS-UP
1977	Manchester United	2-1	Liverpool
1978	Ipswich Town	1-0	Arsenal
1979	Arsenal	3-2 (aet)	Manchester United
1980	West Ham United	1-0	Arsenal
1981	Tottenham Hotspur	1-1 (aet), 3-2	Manchester City
1982	Tottenham Hotspur	1-1 (aet), 1-0	QPR
1983	Manchester United	2-2 (aet), 4-0	Brighton & Hove A
1984	Everton	2-0	Watford
1985	Manchester United	1-0 (aet)	Everton
1986	Liverpool	3-1	Everton
1987	Coventry City	3-2 (aet)	Tottenham Hotspur
1988	Wimbledon	1-0	Liverpool
1989	Liverpool	3-2 (aet)	Everton
1990	Manchester United	3-3 (aet), 1-0	Crystal Palace
1991	Tottenham Hotspur	2-1 (aet)	Nottingham Forest
1992	Liverpool	2-0	Sunderland
1993	Arsenal	1-1 (aet), 2-1 (aet)	Sheffield Wednesday
1994	Manchester United	4-0	Chelsea
1995	Everton	1-0	Manchester United
1996	Manchester United	1-0	Liverpool
1997	Chelsea	2-0	Middlesbrough
1998	Arsenal	2-0	Newcastle United
1999	Manchester United	2-0	Newcastle United
2000	Chelsea	1-0	Aston Villa
2001	Liverpool	2-1	Arsenal
2002	Arsenal	2-0	Chelsea
2003	Arsenal	1-0	Southampton
2004	Manchester United	3-0	Millwall

The League Cup

Prior to being staged at Wembley in 1967 (and currently at Cardiff), this was played as a two-leg Final.
Sponsors have included Littlewoods, Milk, Rumbelows, Coca-Cola and Worthington

YEAR	WINNERS		RUNNERS-UP
1961	Aston Villa	0-2, 3-0 (aet)	Rotherham United
1962	Norwich City	3-0, 1-0	Rochdale
1963	Birmingham City	3-1, 0-0	Aston Villa
1964	Leicester City	1-1, 3-2	Stoke City
1965	Chelsea	3-2, 0-0	Leicester City
1966	West Brom	1-2, 4-1	West Ham Utd
1967	QPR	3-2	West Brom
1968	Leeds United	1-0	Arsenal
1969	Swindon Town	3-1 (aet)	Arsenal
1970	Manchester City	2-1 (aet)	West Brom
1971	Tottenham Hotspur	2-0	Aston Villa
1972	Stoke City	2-1	Chelsea

YEAR	WINNERS		RUNNERS-UP
1973	Tottenham Hotspur	1-0	Norwich City
1974	Wolves	2-1	Manchester City
1975	Aston Villa	1-0	Norwich City
1976	Manchester City	2-1	Newcastle United
1977	Aston Villa	0-0, 1-1 (aet), 3-2 (aet)	Everton
1978	Nottingham Forest	0-0 (aet), 1-0	Liverpool
1979	Nottingham Forest	3-2	Southampton
1980	Wolves	1-0	Nottingham Forest
1981	Liverpool	1-1 (aet), 2-1	West Ham United
1982	Liverpool	3-1 (aet)	Tottenham Hotspur

• Above
Third Division giant-killers Swindon Town celebrate, 1969.

YEAR	WINNERS		RUNNERS-UP
1983	Liverpool	2-1 (aet)	Manchester United
1984	Liverpool	0-0 (aet), 1-0	Everton
1985	Norwich City	1-0	Sunderland
1986	Oxford United	3-0	QPR
1987	Arsenal	2-1	Liverpool
1988	Luton Town	3-2	Arsenal
1989	Nottingham Forest	3-1	Luton Town
1990	Nottingham Forest	1-0	Oldham Athletic
1991	Sheffield Wednesday	1-0	Manchester United
1992	Manchester United	1-0	Nottingham Forest
1993	Arsenal	2-1	Sheffield Wednesday
1994	Aston Villa	3-1	Manchester United

YEAR	WINNERS		RUNNERS-UP
1995	Liverpool	2-1	Bolton Wanderers
1996	Aston Villa	3-0	Leeds United
1997	Leicester City	1-1 (aet), 1-0	Middlesbrough
1998	Chelsea	2-0 (aet)	Middlesbrough
1999	Tottenham Hotspur	1-0	Leicester City
2000	Leicester City	2-1	Tranmere Rovers
2001	Liverpool	1-1 (aet), Pens 4-3	Birmingham City
2002	Blackburn Rovers	2-1	Tottenham Hotspur
2003	Liverpool	2-0	Manchester United
2004	Middlesbrough	2-0	Bolton Wanderers

European Champions League (previously European Cup)

1956	Real Madrid
1957	Real Madrid
1958	Real Madrid
1959	Real Madrid
1960	Real Madrid
1961	Benfica
1962	Benfica
1963	AC Milan
1964	Internazionale
1965	Internazionale
1966	Real Madrid
1967	Glasgow Celtic
1968	Manchester United
1969	AC Milan
1970	Feyenoord
1971	Ajax
1972	Ajax
1973	Ajax
1974	Bayern Munich
1975	Bayern Munich
1976	Bayern Munich
1977	Liverpool
1978	Liverpool
1979	Nottingham Forest
1980	Nottingham Forest
1981	Liverpool
1982	Aston Villa
1983	SV Hamburg
1984	Liverpool
1985	Juventus
1986	Steaua Bucharest
1987	FC Porto
1988	PSV Eindhoven
1989	AC Milan
1990	AC Milan
1991	Red Star Belgrade
1992	Barcelona
1993	Marseille
1994	AC Milan
1995	Ajax
1996	Juventus
1997	Borussia Dortmund

1998	Real Madrid
1999	Manchester United
2000	Real Madrid
2001	Bayern Munich
2002	Real Madrid
2003	AC Milan
2004	Porto

• Left
Chelsea's Eidur Gudjohnsen (22) hugs teammate Frank Lampard as Arsenal's Robert Pires walks off the field after Chelsea defeated Arsenal during their 2004 Champions League quarter-final.

European Cup Winners' Cup

1961	Fiorentina
1962	Athletico Madrid
1963	Tottenham Hotspur
1964	Sporting Lisbon
1965	West Ham United
1966	Borussia Dortmund
1967	Bayern Munich
1968	AC Milan
1969	Slovan Bratislava
1970	Manchester City
1971	Chelsea
1972	Glasgow Rangers
1973	AC Milan
1974	FC Magdeburg
1975	Kiev Dynamo
1976	Anderlecht
1977	SV Hamburg
1978	Anderlecht
1979	Barcelona
1980	Valencia
1981	Dinamo Tbilisi
1982	Barcelona
1983	Aberdeen
1984	Juventus
1985	Everton
1986	Kiev Dynamo
1987	Ajax
1988	Mechelen
1989	Barcelona
1990	Sampdoria
1991	Manchester United
1992	Werder Bremen
1993	Parma
1994	Arsenal
1995	Real Zaragoza
1996	Paris St Germain
1997	Barcelona
1998	Chelsea
1999	Lazio
(Competition ceased)	

UEFA Cup (Fairs Cup 1858-72)

1958	Barcelona
1960	Barcelona
1961	Roma
1962	Valencia
1963	Valencia
1964	Real Zaragoza
1965	Ferencvaros
1966	Barcelona
1967	Dinamo Zagreb
1968	Leeds
1969	Newcastle
1970	Arsenal
1971	Leeds
1972	Tottenham Hotspur
1973	Liverpool
1974	Feyenoord
1975	Borussia Moenchengladbach
1976	Liverpool
1977	Juventus
1978	PSV Eindhoven
1979	Borussia Moenchengladbach
1980	Eintracht Frankfurt
1981	Ipswich Town
1982	IFK Gothenburg
1983	Anderlecht
1984	Tottenham Hotspur
1985	Real Madrid
1986	Real Madrid
1987	IFK Gothenburg
1988	Bayer Leverkusen
1989	Napoli
1990	Juventus
1991	Inte Milan
1992	Ajax
1993	Juventus
1994	Inter Milan
1995	Parma
1996	Bayern Munich
1997	Schalke 04
1998	Inter Milan
1999	Parma
2000	Galatasaray
2001	Liverpool
2002	Feyenoord
2003	Porto
2004	Valencia

• **Right**
Winners Galatasaray celebrate, 2000.

European Championship (European Nations Cup 1960-68)

1960	Soviet Union
1964	Spain
1968	Italy
1972	West Germany
1976	Czechoslovakia
1980	West Germany

1984	France
1988	Holland
1992	Denmark
1996	Germany
2000	France
2004	Greece

World Cup

1930	Uruguay	4-2	Argentina
1934	Italy	2-1	Czechoslovakia
1938	Italy	4-2	Hungary
1950	Uruguay	2-1	Brazil
1954	West Germany	3-2	Hungary
1958	Brazil	5-2	Sweden
1962	Brazil	3-1	Czechoslovakia
1966	England	4-2	Germany
1970	Brazil	4-1	Italy
1974	West Germany	2-1	Holland
1978	Argentina	3-1	Holland
1982	Italy	3-1	West Germany
1986	Argentina	3-2	West Germany
1990	West Germany	1-0	Argentina
1994	Brazil	0-0	Italy (Brazil won on penalties)
1998	France	3-0	Brazil
2002	Brazil	2-0	Germany

• **Above**

Jules Rimet (left) and the first World Cup that bore his name.

• **Left**

Winning captain Bobby Moore, 1966.

• **Right**

England's Terry Butcher jumps with Pereira and Pachaco of Portugal during their World Cup match in Mexico, 1986. Portugal won 1-0.

Index

The pictures in this book
were provided courtesy of:

GETTY IMAGES,

101 Bayham Street, London NW1 0AG.

1

POPPERFOTO

The Old Mill, Overstone Farm, Northampton NN6 0AB

Design and artwork by Darren Roberts.

Layout and editorial design by Simon Joslin, Creative Visual Communication.

Series Editors Jules Gammond and Tim Exell.

Proofread by Alan Kinsman.

Written by Michael Heatley, with valued assistance from Graham Betts, Chris Mason and Dennis Turner. Thanks also to PRC Publishing for permission to quote from Michael Heatley's Pictorial History Of Soccer in Chapter 1: Origins of the Game.